Puppet-Assisted Pla

Puppet-Assisted Play Therapy is an innovative and comprehensive approach that significantly advances the field of play therapy. This easy to read, user-friendly book includes history, creative interventions, case studies, the art of puppetry, and the worldwide benefits of puppet-assisted play therapy. It includes instructions for making customized puppets for a therapist's practice and original research on the relationship of puppet therapy on children's creativity. By describing all the various facets of puppet-assisted play therapy, this engaging text explores how using puppets produces a powerful connection and trust needed to implement the therapeutic process.

Puppet-Assisted Play Therapy is a valuable addition to the library of any therapist, social worker, counsellor, teacher, or other professional interested in play and puppets with children.

Cheryl Hulburd, MSW, RSW, CPT, RPT, is a certified EMDR therapist and certified and registered play therapist who lives, works, and plays in British Columbia, Canada.

Puppet-Assisted Play Therapy

Theory, Research, and Practice

Cheryl Hulburd

Routledge
Taylor & Francis Group

LONDON AND NEW YORK

First published 2021 by Routledge

2 Park Square, Milton Park, Abingdon, Oxon OX14 4RN

605 Third Avenue, New York, NY 10017

Routledge is an imprint of the Taylor & Francis Group, an informa business

First issued in paperback 2022

Publisher's Note

The publisher has gone to great lengths to ensure the quality of this reprint but
points out that some imperfections in the original copies may be apparent.

Library of Congress Cataloging-in-Publication Data
A catalog record for this title has been requested

ISBN: 978-0-367-33188-7 (hbk)
ISBN: 978-1-03-233592-6 (pbk)
DOI: 10.4324/9780429319648

Typeset in Times New Roman
by Newgen Publishing UK

MIX
Paper | Supporting
responsible forestry
FSC
www.fsc.org FSC™ C013985

Printed in the United Kingdom
by Henry Ling Limited

Dedicated in loving memory to my mother,
Sylvia Ann Boksenbaum (1942–1988)

Contents

Figures

Acknowledgments

I would like to thank the following for their inspiration, help, and support. Without them this book would never have come to fruition. I am grateful to the people who helped me successfully complete this book: Desiree Ingram, Jill Fuller Gibson, Jared Howe, and Gabriella Escobar Ari. Their extraordinary skill set and expertise made this possible.

I would also like to thank those who provided me with the impetus that prompted the conception of this project: Alejandro Aguavil Aguavil, Diana Neiman, Dorian Turner, Ann Stockman, Carolynn Schubert, Sheila Davis and in loving memory, my beloved friend, Doreen Oosterhaus.

My daughter, Sylvie Ann Hulburd, helped initiate my focus and interest with puppets and ventriloquism. A special thank you goes out to my husband, Barry J. Hulburd, for his continued encouragement and of course, my cotherapists, Herman, Bear-niece, Peter, Bryan, Betsy and Lucy.

Introduction

While conducting workshops and training seminars on puppet-assisted play therapy (PAPT®) in the United States and Canada, I often hear educators and mental health practitioners say that they are aware of the booming interest in puppets but have no idea how to effectively integrate them into their own practices.

Puppet play provides a way for children to conquer fear, heal from past trauma, and play through difficult social situations. Puppet play allows children to put distance between themselves and their emotions, and to take control of situations that they may not be able to influence in real life. Puppet play allows children to feel a sense of self-control and develop skills that they can then put into practice in their everyday lives.

This book is an innovative and comprehensive guide to the field of PAPT. It is intended to help you become more effective, fun, and creative in your practice with children. This book includes discussions of relevant history, theory, research, practice, case studies, specific creative therapeutic interventions, and the art of puppetry. The unique techniques that I provide here allow for personalization based on the therapist's personality and creativity.

Let me first introduce Herman the Turtle as my cotherapist puppet. Herman is a "So-Shell worker" and a member of the British Columbia Association for So-Shell Workers. His certificate of merit hangs in my office, and he has become well known in my practice. The children that I work with call my office "Herman's House."

It is my intent that this book will assist not only therapists, but anyone interested in working with children, including art therapists, drama therapists, filial play therapists, coaches, and mentors. The presented information and techniques can also aid child care workers, clinical/ social workers, counselors, learning assistants, nursery and primary teachers, nurses, occupational therapists, pediatricians, psychiatrists, psychologists, special needs teachers, and other professionals who are

Figure 0.1 Herman's So-Shell Worker Certificate of Merit

training to work with children and wish to acquire or enhance play therapy skills.

Throughout this book, I also answer the questions that are commonly asked by the numerous mental health practitioners and educators who already include puppets in their repertoire of toys. I recommend specific techniques for the various therapy components (e.g., engagement, assessment intervention, and terminations), including processing questions, dialogue, and games for use in treatment plans.

This information is intended to help you and your practice become more effective, fun, and creative when working with children. The concepts presented are applicable to all aspects of the therapeutic process. My wish is that you and the children will benefit from the wonderful art of puppetry and PAPT.

1   History of Puppetry

Researchers have used the fun theory to explain human behavior throughout history. Volkswagen conducted a research study at a busy Stockholm train station during rush hour. (Fun theory study: www.youtube.com/results?search_query=vw+fun+theory)

The passengers exited the station via a double stairway with a railing down the middle; an escalator ran up one side, with a regular stairway on the other. The researchers wired the stairs to look and sound like piano keys. They aimed to determine whether more people would take the stairs, thereby getting more exercise, if it was fun to do. Photos of the experiment showed children dancing up and down the steps, dogs exploring, and commuters smiling as they enjoyed this unique creation. The results indicated that 66% more people than normal chose the stairs over the escalator. There was evidence that fun changes behavior for the better – otherwise known as the fun theory.

Researchers have used the fun theory to explain human behavior throughout history. Puppetry is an example of a tradition that is explainable by the fun theory. Puppetry is an ancient art form that has been part of performances, ceremonies, and celebrations for centuries. In *Puppetry: A World History*, Blumenthal (2005) cited one source placing puppetry's birthplace in India around 1000 BC. Archaeologists uncovered stick puppets that performers used to dramatize Indian epic texts and make them entertaining for the masses. In Indonesia, *walang* puppet shows opened with a speech from a holy person; such shows were treated with a certain degree of seriousness.

Blumenthal documented that the earliest record of a puppet performance was in hieroglyphs from the Nile Basin six centuries before the reign of Tutankhamen. Archaeologists have also found figures and statues with movable limbs and parts in tombs from early Middle Eastern civilizations.

Puppetry as an art form dates back to the ancient societies of Egypt and Greece (Blumenthal, 2005), as well as various Native American cultures (Malkin, 1977). Puppet shows in 17th-century Europe and Asia were quite popular and well respected. The use of puppets as a therapeutic tool was not introduced until the 20th century. As early as the 1920s, Klein (1929, as cited in Sweeney, 2009) noted that children used puppets, among other objects, to express their inner feelings and personify people in their lives. By the 1930s, Woltmann (1951) had documented the use of puppet shows as a psychotherapeutic intervention with hospitalized children.

Woltmann (1940) described puppets as useful for a therapeutic context because they provide opportunities for spontaneity, are easily manipulated, and lend themselves naturally to a symbolic process of self-expression. Puppet play creates an absorbing atmosphere of fantasy for the child, while at the same time being nonthreatening (Haworth, 1968). Children are able to identify with the characters involved in puppet play and project their feelings and interpersonal conflicts onto them. In this way, children can better communicate their distress, without having to directly claim traumatic experiences and painful emotions as their own (Haworth, 1968). In turn, the therapist can use puppets to express understanding and provide corrective emotional experiences (Kaduson & Schaefer, 1997). Sweeney and Homeyer (1999) cited Woltmann's conclusion that "in structured puppet show presentations, each child in the audience identifies with characters and action. Although situations presented may be threatening, everything is still make believe, thereby creating safety for the child" (p. 268).

Rambert (as cited in Philpott, 1977) from Switzerland compared the use of dolls and puppets in play therapy, concluding that puppets were more useful. She explained her reasoning as such:

> A puppet can be handled more easily, is more robust, resists beating much more, and the most important fact, that a child can completely disappear behind the guignol's (puppet's) personality as he enters it completely, inhabits it, so to speak. Even without a curtain to hide behind—a formal stage—a child identifies himself easily with a puppet or gives it the personality of one of the family and makes it move and talk in a great variety of characterizations. The puppet method proved so useful that many severe neuroses could be cured quickly, in less time than with any other way.
>
> (Philpott, 1977, p. 11)

At the same time, without being aware of Rambert's work, Woltmann, a psychologist and assistant to a doctor at the Bellevue Hospital in New York, started a puppet theater at the hospital's ward for maladjusted and neurotic children. During daily sequences and group and individual treatments, he encouraged the children to react and talk and act out their behavior (Philpott, 1977).

Woltmann began puppet play in 1935, and it soon became a routine technique in child psychoanalysis. His interest in the therapeutic possibilities of puppets began in 1931 when he "made a couple of potato-head characters to amuse his ailing stepdaughter and hastened her recovery" (Woltmann, 1951, p. 141). He explained that when children performed with puppets, they often unintentionally revealed their mental or emotional states. Indeed, verbal exchanges between puppet characters and the audience can be very revealing.

Rochelle Ginis (as cited in Philpott, 1977) explained that "animation" goes beyond mere "manipulation," as "puppets have the inherent ability to portray inhibitions and fears" (p. 140). Gendler (1986) conducted puppetry therapy with small groups of children and proposed several therapeutic objectives in using puppetry, including psychological safety in expressing denied feelings or discussing unspeakable events (see Sweeney & Homeyer, 1999; Woltmann, 1951).

Irwin (1985) used puppets in their work with families to observe communication patterns and decision-making strategies. Sweeney and Homeyer (1999) contended:

> ...the use of puppets in transitional objects serve as a developmental tool to allow children to bridge the gap between reality and fantasy. Hence, puppetry is developmentally appropriate for younger children. In therapy, in enhancing the group process, puppets provide a vehicle for developing empathy and support among group members and enable the expression of deep conflicts through the pooling of unconscious needs. Children in groups serve as alter egos to each other through the repetition of puppet play solutions to problems will often develop and gain momentum.
>
> (p. 268)

Irwin and Shapiro (1975) developed a method for diagnosing children through their puppet play, as well as using puppetry as a therapeutic technique. Their method is discussed in greater detail in Chapter 5.

Puppets in therapy were further developed by Anna Freud, who adapted her father's methods to treat the children with whom she worked. She asserted that a child's neurosis can be healed by "dramatization." She initiated "play therapy," wherein children illustrate their inner conflicts "by way of toys, dolls, sand, plasticine, etc. most of the time without realizing at all what was being revealed" (Marcus, as cited in Philpott, 1977, p. 11).

In 1960, Turnbull (as cited in Philpott, 1977) wrote that puppetry "is one of the few activities of which they never tire" (p. 13). Marcus discussed therapeutic puppetry in the 1948 *Puppet Post*, writing, "We had practically no failure. All patients were at least much better, few relapsed and about 40% cured completely, as their parents' letters testify a year or two after the cure" (Philpott, 1977, p. 12).

More information on the history of puppetry may be found in Philpott's (1977) *Puppets and Therapy,* in which the author synthesizes an informal collection of reports, articles, commentary, and reviews about various aspects of this field. The topics include deaf children, the handicapped and mentally challenged population, and diagnostics, with numerous supplemented case histories.

Puppetry has remained a thriving art form in modern-day culture, serving as a medium to communicate, entertain, challenge ideas, and assist with therapy. Television uses puppets for education. Bible studies use puppets to illustrate scripture. Some cultures use ceremonial puppets to portray spiritual topics. Many mental health professionals now use puppetry in their daily practices. There is a growing worldwide interest in using puppets with children, and I predict that the practice will continue to expand in popularity as knowledge of PAPT disseminates throughout healing and educational communities.

2 PAPT and Neurobiology Constructs

Researchers suggest that the most important aspect of effective therapy, regardless of the approach or modality, is the therapist's empathetic nature and the connection between patient and therapist. Puppets enhance this connection. The reason that PAPT can effectively reach troubled children and their families when other methods cannot has its basis in established neurobiology research.

PAPT and Integration

Puppetry's positive neurobiological effects come from its impact on the whole brain. Recent researchers have supported the theory that good mental health results from a harmonious integration of all brain areas: right brain, left brain, upper brain, and lower (reptilian) brain. The right brain hemisphere performs holistic and nonlinear processing that is responsible for visual and spatial information. The right hemisphere accounts for all emotions, feeling, sensations, images, and creativity. In contrast, the left brain hemisphere is responsible for the "L" functions: logic, linearity, language, and literal (Siegel & Hartzell, 2003). Through this processing, the brain translates information into predictable cause-and-effect patterns. The left brain processes mathematical, factual, and straightforward information.

Dr. Daniel Siegel, a leading expert in neurobiology and psychology, described the two hemispheres as riverbanks in a metaphorical diagram of the brain. The left brain, a rigid producer of logical conclusions, can be represented by the left bank of the river. This side of the brain inhibits connection with others. Mr. Spock from *Star Trek* lives solely in the left brain; he has no capacity to love, feel, or empathize. Mr. Spock's focus is limited and focused on rules, structure, and regulation.

The right brain, represented by the right bank of Dr. Siegel's metaphorical river, is artistic, free-flowing, and looks chaotic. This part of the brain is responsible for social understanding. An example of relying solely on the right brain would be Jim Carrey performing a silly persona, without any factual information affecting his decisions or actions. Another example would be a person fully involved in the art world; exploring, creating, experiencing, yet they forget to pay their bills.

Being stuck on one bank or the other creates problems with functioning. One edge of the spectrum is rigid, and the other is chaotic. Integration, however, helps the distinct parts of the brain work together as a whole. Within the body, the lungs breathe, the heart pumps blood, and the stomach digests food; each part needs to do its individual job, but all organs must also work as a whole.

Using the river metaphor, when both hemispheres are integrated, Siegel and Bryson (2011) described the middle of the river as the "river of wellbeing" (p. 11). Siegel explains that within the river of wellbeing, both right and left brain are integrated. One can make sense out of emotion, and the left hemisphere can create logical meaning from the information that it receives from the right hemisphere. When logic is applied to feelings, the brain begins to become integrated.

Siegel and Bryson (2011) contended that a mentally healthy person floats in the middle of the river, rather than being stranded on either side of the riverbank. The terms *go with the flow*, *be stable*, and *well-balanced* all represent being in the middle of the river. The two hemispheres are considered vertically integrated; however, horizontal integration is also important. Horizontal integration consists of the lower, or reptilian brain (sometimes referred to as the primitive brain), and the upper, or higher brain. This reptilian brain promotes survival by reacting instinctively to a detected threat, as a reptile or other animal might.

In the context of therapy, it is important to note that threats can be perceived both physically and/or emotionally; the reptilian brain reacts to both kinds of threats. As an example of a physical threat, when a finger touches a hot stove, an instant reaction without emotion is activated. This would classify as the flight response. As an example of an emotional threat, when a man in a dark parking lot appears from behind a corner, one experiences the flight, fight, or freeze response.

The upper brain develops in early life and continues to develop actively into early adulthood. Planning, thinking, and imagining are the complex processes of the higher brain. This allows for control over emotions, self-understanding, morality, empathy, and sound decision making. Optimal development of the upper brain comes with repeated use and practice.

Siegel and Bryson (2011) explained that engaging both the upper and lower brain results in horizontal integration. The integration occurs when the upper brain thoughtfully considers actions based on the reaction of the lower reptilian brain. This involves thinking before acting, instead of acting before thinking. Siegel referred to this connection as the *mental staircase*. The upstairs (i.e., higher brain) and the downstairs (i.e., lower brain) must work together. When a child's mental staircase is well integrated, they are better able to regulate emotions, think before acting, consider consequences, and be empathetic.

Siegel and Bryson (2011) explained two therapeutic techniques to integrate the whole brain. The first technique is called "connect and redirect" (Siegel & Bryson, 2011, p. 22). The therapist connects with the patient through the right side of the brain. After connecting with the patient, the therapist can use the left brain to redirect them and provide logical explanations.

A child who is angry and kicks another child is more responsive if the therapist connects with them first by validating feelings – "I know you're angry." Following the connection, the therapist can redirect the child by suggesting verbal expressions of feelings instead. The child is more likely to hear, to learn, and to follow through than if the therapist simply demanded a redirection. Through connection and then redirection, it is possible to achieve integration (Siegel & Bryson, 2011).

Siegel and Bryson (2011) referred to the second technique used to integrate the brain as "name it to tame it" (*it* refers to an emotion). Engagement of the whole brain occurs by putting the facts of the experience in order and thus the experience into words. Then the right brain revisits the emotions felt (Siegel & Bryson, 2011). Children can cope with their big, scary right brain feelings if someone can help them use their left brain to make sense of what's going on and put things in order. According to these authors, "merely assigning a name or label to what we feel literally calms down the activity of the emotional circuitry in the right hemisphere" (Siegel & Bryson, 2011, p. 29).

A very effective way to enhance this integration is through PAPT. Puppet-assisted play therapy addresses both vertical and horizontal integration. The right hemisphere is addressed when a child initially meets the puppet by evoking feelings of fun, connection, and enjoyment. Further interactions or validating feelings may elicit past experiences that arouse other emotions. The left hemisphere is addressed when the puppet talks to them by reviewing the experience with them and suggesting reasons, perspectives, or solutions that explain the experience. The upper brain and lower brain work together when the puppet models expressing empathy, regulating emotions, and considering consequences. Whole brain integration is like listening to a concert when all the instruments are playing in harmony simultaneously, or watching a meaningful, well-thought-out puppet show performed by emotionally charged characters.

PAPT and Memory

In addition to integration, work with memory is essential in helping a troubled child. Once again, PAPT is perfectly tailored to this task. Memory functions based on linkages in the brain between experiences, ideas, and images from the past. The brain saves these links as neural pathways. A neural pathway can be envisioned as a set of ski tracks in fresh snow. Every memory, behavior, or action that follows in this track deepens the track further. When children have a difficult or traumatic experience, this track can become the default path.

If a dog bites a child, it is likely that the child will fear all dogs. Regardless of whether or not the next dog that the child encounters is aggressive, the child will be affected by their experiences with the previous dog. Every time the child avoids a dog, the repetition of avoidance strengthens and deepens this neural pathway. The deeper the track, the more automatic this experience becomes. The memory is stored in both the brain and body. The reaction of fear will continue to manifest around strange dogs; without intervention, the child may avoid dogs their entire life.

Past experiences strongly influence present perceptions and feelings. The goal is to help troubled children create a new memory as the default track, instead of the older one that is causing them problems.

Figure 2.1 Ski tracks illustrating neuroplasticity

Figure 2.2 Implicit memory (inside) – explicit memory (outside)

There are two kinds of memories: implicit memory and explicit memory. The photo below provides mnemonics for these two different types.

Implicit memory can be thought of as "inside" memories. We don't think about implicit memories; they are subconscious, like steering a car on the highway, knowing where we live, or remembering our family. Implicit memories can be developed as early as the preverbal stage. These preverbal stage memories create the default path.

Explicit memories are memories that are in our conscious awareness. These include what we ate for dinner, how our weekend was, or which hike we prefer. These explicit memories are "ex," or outside of, our automatic memories. As Siegel (1999) explained:

> If events are overwhelming and filled with terror, a number of factors may inhibit the hippocampal processing of explicit memory, and therefore may block explicit encoding and subsequent retrieval. Such factors include divided attention, amygdala discharge, and release of noradrenaline and corticosteroids in response to massive stress. Such conditions allow implicit memory to be encoded while explicit processing is impaired.

(p. 47)

When implicit or subconscious memories evolve into explicit or conscious memories, a new experience is created. Every new experience results in a memory that literally changes the physical makeup of the brain, as neurons are constantly connecting based on our experiences.

Neuroscientists explain this process with the phrase, "Neurons that fire together, wire together." Every new experience causes certain neurons to fire, and when they do, they link up with other neurons that are firing at the same time. Once memories form, they shape our perceptions by using associations in the brain to anticipate what will happen next.

The neurons that fire together when a child gets bit by the dog may be feelings of fear and a reaction to run. If this child's mom was baking cookies at the time of the attack, the smell of the cookies may have been wired into this neural pathway as well. Hence, if this child smells similar cookies baking, his reflexes may cause him to become anxious, have an increased heart rate, and shake. Such triggers cause symptomatic manifestations that are confusing for those that experience them. These are repeating patterns, and no amount of logic is going to change the experience until some of the implicit wounds are healed.

PAPT and Brain Integration

By reenacting unpleasant incidents in the playroom, therapists can create the distance from emotions necessary for children to process them. Therapists use puppets to address the upper brain by reenacting the previous threat, danger, or negative experience, as well as to regulate emotions of the lower reptilian brain. This practice often incorporates additional intervening puppets. For example, the therapist's puppet may validate, confirm, or suggest alternative solutions.

Using puppets, therapists can create new experiences surrounding the original incident of distress. As Badenoch (2008) explained,

> From the beginning the playroom provides a novel situation and the therapist gives ample permission for the child to explore freely. Often, this open environment activates what neuroscientist Jaak Pankeepp (1998) calls the *seeking circuits*—one of seven genetically based motivational circuits residing in our limbic regions of the brain. Three of them—rage, fear, and separation distress—become activated when children are out of connection with adults. The other four—caring, social bonding, playfulness, and seeking—arise under conditions of warm, contingent connection (Sunderland, 2006). Once it has been activated by novelty, the seeking system supports the release of dopamine (among other brain chemicals), which cascades through the frontal lobes, providing the sense of enjoyment, focus, and purpose to see something through. We can imagine that children in the playroom and a safe adult might find speedy access to the seeking system.
>
> (p. 301)

Hence, this access is elevated through puppet play due to the combination of connection and novelty. One of the most powerful ways in which our brains integrate isolated neural networks is in generating coherent stories about our lives (Badenoch, 2008). When we experience and integrate a novel situation, the brain creates a new coherent story with positive healing qualities in the memory. This integration adds to the coherent story of our lives, thereby altering and healing the memory.

Integration Techniques

To review, it is possible to facilitate brain integration through Siegel and Bryson's (2011) recommendations: (a) name it to tame it and (b) connect to redirect. Puppets are talented at these skills. Role modeling can be performed by your cotherapist puppet with ease and proficiency. Therapists may use puppet interactions that implement these techniques to achieve right brain and left brain integration into a single "river of well-being." When two puppets talk to each other, the element of personal vulnerability is mitigated, thereby enabling easier and calmer integration.

Integrating Spontaneity and Creativity

Children's language is play, and toys are their words. Puppets are great toys that children can use to both play and communicate. Puppets may enhance children's spontaneity and creativity, which results in squirts of the neurotransmitter dopamine. Brain cells receive dopamine when experiencing something pleasant, thereby motivating the individual to seek out the experience again.

Puppet-assisted play therapy also creates neuroplasticity. Fostering integration of whole brain memories through puppets creates new experiences. These new experiences create new attitudes, beliefs, and behaviors. The brain physically changes in response to new experiences – demonstrating neuroplasticity.

When children take control over what is happening in their brain, they can begin to reframe their experiences and feelings. Since implicit memories can also create fear, avoidance, sadness, and other painful emotions and bodily sensations, PAPT can help children convert and reframe implicit memories to explicit memories. The integration of these memories brings insight, understanding, and healing. This transformation is evident through the presentation of healing children who are involved in PAPT.

Puppetry is a fun and engaging technique that enables children to better integrate their experiences. Parents can use puppets at home to continue the reenactment and help children process events outside the therapeutic session. The advantage of PAPT over other therapies is that everyone can have puppets at home. Puppets provide a safe environment for children to recount their experiences. Puppetry also allows children to process an event or experience in a less threatening way. This is because the use of puppets creates a distance from the child's actual story. Puppets are a medium that incorporates only one part of the child – their hand. Ingram (Personal communication, 2009) explained that people puppets are once removed from a child's psyche, while animal puppets are twice removed. Objects such as flower puppets can be three times removed.

Memories are about associations, of which the brain is the mechanism. The brain processes something in the present moment and links it with an experience from the past. This strongly influences how we understand what we see or feel in the present. During any experience, neurons fire together or become activated with new signals. Neurons that fire together, wire together.

In summary, memories shape our current perceptions by causing us to anticipate what will happen next. The past shapes the present via associations in the brain due to the two different types of memory. PAPT changes the brain by creating new experiences, memories, and neural pathways thereby encouraging happy, healthy children. Like the ski tacks in the fresh snow, new tracks or memories developed during PAPT create a different experience. These new tracks create a changed slope, a new freedom, and a new path

3 Puppetry Enhances Creativity

My favorite Albert Einstein quote is, "Imagination is more important than knowledge." All of the information in the world is only as valuable as the creative use of that information. Creativity is a paramount foundation for positive mental health. Gowan et al. (1967) asserted that "Creativity involves a fundamental change in personality structure" (p. 25). They continued, "Creativity is a universal characteristic of self-actualizing people. This form of creativeness reaches beyond special talent—creativeness; it is a fundamental characteristic of human nature. It touches whatever activity the healthy person is engaged in" (Gowan et al., 1967, p. 26).

One major component of improving children's mental health that is missing from today's society is the promotion of creativity. Creativity is crucial for healthy child development; however, it is severely undervalued, and some mental health professionals do not believe that it can be enhanced. I posit, however, that puppetry can assist in alleviating this crisis by fostering creative potential in children.

Last year, I treated a child with a lack of self-regulation – a common symptom of trauma. As the child created a superhero puppet, he noticed a red button on the puppet's outfit. Of course, this button contained magic powers. The child pressed the puppet's button when he needed to self-regulate. As the child practiced pressing his newfound button regulator throughout the course of his storytelling, he developed his own internal mechanisms to calm himself. We then created a button for him to place in his pocket to use at home and at school to regulate himself.

We may not like to admit it, but modern society and culture have conspired to inhibit children's creativity. Many teachers hinder creativity in the classroom by teaching a single way to do or perceive things. For example, while conducting research on creativity in a grade school, I asked the class, "If you gave me two cookies yesterday and two cookies today, how many cookies will I have?" Every child in the classroom answered four cookies, but my response was zero, because

I had eaten all the cookies. They found this surprising. I explained that there are many ways to look at each question. Teaching that there is only one right answer dampens creativity. When students do not follow exact expectations within the classroom, many teachers become upset and correct them.

Media sources such as television, movies, and computers can all diminish creativity. Media also emphasizes a particular standard as "correct." For example, there is one correct shape to be; if you are not the "right" size, you are the "wrong" size. Peer pressure is intrinsic to adolescent behavior and development. When youth are influenced by peer pressure to conform, their creativity is further constrained. Social messages also advocate the seriousness of being "in style" or following trends. Nonconformance is often interpreted as silliness, which may be perceived as eccentricity or abnormality. Nonconformance is also discouraged in modern schools and communities through peer judgment or ridicule.

Singer (as cited in Oaklander, 1978) and others have "statistically [shown] that children who are able to be imaginative have higher IQs and are able to cope better, and that encouraging a child to be imaginative improves his or her ability to cope and learn" (p. 10). Most children are not capable of discussing their problems in the same way as adults. Instead, they express their emotions and unconscious thoughts during their play. Thus, therapeutic tools that facilitate the creative expression of fantasy are incredibly useful when working with this population (Philpott, 1977). PAPT fits this criterion beautifully. By its nature, research on creativity enhancement includes various operational definitions of creativity, which are difficult to compare or rank. Runco (2004) categorized creativity into four components: the creative person, process, product, and press. Press relates to environmental factors such as schools, conditions, instructions, and teachers. The most common measurement of creativity is the Torrance Test for Creative Thinking (Torrance, 1990). TTCT tests the process concept. The process concept of creativity specifically measures students' divergent thinking skills. The results of the TTCT support the improvement of task-specific creativity.

Researchers have provided empirical evidence suggesting that creativity can be enhanced through practice. Others, however, have reported negative findings associated with creativity enhancement. This is largely due to the mixed operational definitions of creativity; that is, such researchers were usually comparing apples to oranges. One argument against creative enhancement questions the probability of a transfer from programs to real-life creativity.

Puppetry is steeped in the marriage of play, storytelling, magical fantasy, and the arts. In 2007, I conducted research with a literature peer review that incorporated six areas: enhancing creativity, benefits of creativity, negative findings, paradoxical latitudes, creative play, and of course, puppetry. I first administered the Torrance Test of Creative Thinking (Torrance, 1990) to students in grades 3 and 4 then developed and taught a creativity enhancement curriculum for eight classes, before retesting the students to measure change in creative thinking. Following program implementation, the school principal conducted the testing, and the Scholastic Test Service performed the scoring (see Appendix A).

The results of my research validated that both creative play and puppetry offer beneficial effects for children's positive development. My findings reflected that divergent thinking, or creativity, fosters healthy development. This healthy development is fueled by enhanced positive personal perceptions, problem-solving skills, conflict resolution skills, communication skills, academic ability, coping skills, resiliency, critical thinking, and social affective domains.

Why, then, do teachers promote convergent thinking? The answer lies in teachers' contradictory attitudes; although interested in enhancing students' creativity, they were also stymied by students' nonconforming ideas disrupting the classroom. Hence, creativity in the classroom represents a practical paradox for many teachers.

The results of my study with grade 3 and 4 students revealed several clear messages to any professionals working with young children:

1. We must encourage children to use their imagination and be creative.
2. Children must think, feel, and act differently in order to solve problems.
3. Creativity gives children reparative experiences.
4. More creativity allows for more freedom.
5. Media and technology are disabling children's imagination and creativity.

This is a perfect opportunity for puppet-assisted play therapy. As Oaklander (1978) stated:

> Through fantasy we can have fun with the child, and we can also find out what a child's process is. Usually his or her fantasy process (how she does things and moves around in her fantasy world) is the same as her life process. We can look into the inner realms of the child's being through fantasy. We can bring out what is kept hidden

or avoided and we can also find out what's going on in the child's life from her perspective. For these reasons we encourage fantasy and use it as a therapeutic tool.

(p. 11)

The above is especially true when using puppets. The enhancement of creativity through puppetry is now well documented.

4   PAPT Addresses Theoretical Platforms

Theoretical platforms are the premise for the various treatments in therapy. Treatments derived from these theories are either directive or nondirective in nature. Directive therapies structure sessions based on the assumption that the training and experience of a therapist equip them to manage the therapeutic process and guide the client. Nondirective therapy sessions are based on a client's lead and self-direction, assuming the client knows where to go and what they need, while the therapist listens, supports, and reflects. A therapist using nondirective play therapy must pay attention to the child's story, discoveries, and what is going on in their therapeutic experience (Oaklander, 1978).

A few nondirective theories include experiential, child-centered/humanistic theory, psychoanalytical and psychodynamic theory, and object relations theory. Both directive and nondirective therapies easily assimilate with PAPT, and are used to address healing, change, and behavior regulation. PAPT facilitates all of these, whether it is used in nondirective or directive play therapy. The approach is dictated by the prescribed needs of the individual client or child.

PAPT and Child-Centered/Humanistic Theory

Landreth (2002) explained child-centered theory or humanistic theory, contending that "the innate human capacity of the child is to strive toward growth and maturity. The premise of this theory is that the child has the ability to be constructively self-directing to reach his or her potential" (p. 65). This potential is influenced by a healing environment, both internal and external.

Rogers and Maslow are two major theorists associated with the humanistic perspective. Rogers' theory of personality and behavior has one basic proposition: that an individual strives to actualize, maintain, and enhance themselves. Self-actualization is a principal that describes the belief that an individual has the capacity for self-direction; "This force may be characterized as a drive toward maturity, independence and self-direction" (Axline, 1947, p. 10). This self-direction is to achieve one's full potential. "The therapist's objective is to relate to the child in ways that will release the child's inner directional, constructive, forward-moving, creative, self-healing power. They are empowered and their developmental capabilities are released for self-exploration and self-discovery, resulting in constructive change" (Landreth, 2002). This principle of self-actualization is in the direction of socialization.

Children can utilize puppets to express, share, and change in relation to their "inner" dynamics. This approach emphasizes an individual's inherent drive towards self-actualization and creativity. The "outer" healing environment is the inherent enticement of playing with puppets.

The framework, the self-initiated activity, evolves from Virginia Axline's (1947) guidelines of *Play Therapy*. This author contended that "the child leads the action or conversation and that the therapist maintains the relationship through acceptance, and permission for the child to express feelings completely. The therapist reflects these expressed emotionalized attitudes back to him in such a way as to help him understand himself a little better." (In the safety of a therapeutic relationship, this healing occurs with creativity and spontaneity.) A child announces, "I am going to make a puppet show," then tells their story through the puppets (Axline, 1947, p. 17).

Child-centered play therapy evolved from humanistic theory. The child's focus is the focus of the session as they lead and direct the session. Mental health is evident in creative outlets and creativity is paramount in child-centered play therapy. Puppet play is creative play and for this reason, it is advantageous to have numerous puppets in your playroom. Animal puppets, human puppets, dinosaur puppets, and monster puppets are exceptional tools in any playroom.

When children play, the therapist reflects their play, their wishes, their needs, and their feelings, as described in Roger's theory. Validation and new insights are accomplished. It is important that playroom toys do not have batteries, hence, puppets are optimal for this creativity.

Strong emotions are elicited when children are testing for protection and confronting disturbing memories. Norton and Norton (1997) posited that children require a strong supportive relationship in order to address their pain. When children begin to play out a traumatic experience, it is painful. Norton and Norton continued:

> A traumatic event is re-enacted through associations, symbols and metaphors, re-approaching their painful emotional experience of

the event in the developmental stage occurring at the onset of the trauma. During this type of play, a child will stop briefly in order to obtain reassurance of the security she has with the therapist. Then, she returns to her fantasy play, this time going to a deeper level. She only confronts, however, as much as she can tolerate at any given moment. Each time this pattern is repeated, the child gains a sense of control, dignity and empowerment (appropriate to her age and development) over that part of her play. She reaches a time when she knows she has conquered the negative emotionality surrounding those parts of her emotional experience. In essence, she is reframing her experiences with a restored sense of empowerment, dignity, and control. It is during this process that healing occurs.

(p. 22)

The therapist allows the child to address her pain by letting the child lead the way. This is the essence of experiential child-centered therapy. The child is central to the direction of how the play session unfolds. Hence, "Children allowed to direct their own therapy are able to *reframe* the experiences of their trauma, resulting in a restored sense of well-being" (Norton & Norton, 1997, p. 12).

In my playroom, Johnny, from a domestic violent household, experienced this new reframe of experience. He chose a mad angry puppet tiger to play with. His tiger roared through the playroom terrorizing Betsy, my service dog. Betsy began barking. I asked Johnny what he thought Betsy might be saying to him. He said she was scared. Herman, my cotherapist turtle puppet, concurred that he was scared. I joined in as well and admitted that I was scared too. I asked Johnny what we should do. He responded that maybe the tiger should stop roaring and growling. I asked: "So, you can decide to stop his growling, so we won't be scared?" He answered: "Yes, anyone can decide to stop being scary."

The next session Johnny walked in and said he was mad and angry and thought it best that Betsy leave the playroom this week. Again, I questioned him. I said: So, you can decide when you act angry and you can stop if you know it is hurting or scaring someone? He had an AHA moment. He understood that scary angry behavior is a choice and he could choose to stop if he decided that was the best thing to do. What a message for a little boy whose role model is abuse. He learned early that abusive behavior is a choice that can be altered.

Dr. G. Landreth, the founder of the Center for Play Therapy in Denton, Texas expands on Norton and Norton's (1997) ideas. Landreth

(2002) explains that following this healing play, the child does not forget the event, yet can remember it with a positive outlook. The experience becomes a new memory, a part of their life that they now have control over, that they can move forward from with confidence. The objective was not to solve the problem, rather to encourage a sense of well being where they can resolve issues with a feeling of control and understanding.

Another example of healing play happened in my playroom with Jill. Jill came to therapy after suffering severe abuse from her biological mother. Her adopted mother brought her in due to unregulated behavior in kindergarten. She chose two puppets to play with and had one puppet attacking the other. Repetitive play ensued for several sessions. She then took off the attacker puppet, threw it on the floor and began stomping on it. She verbalized that the puppet who attacked was now dead.

Jill stomped over to the easel, painted black paint on the paper and then flicked paint throughout the playroom. Herman asked: "Can you tell me about this?" She said "the city was destroyed and got wiped out in a battle." She picked up a water spray bottle, handed me the paper towels and said: "Follow me. I will squirt [with the sprayer] and you wipe it up." The mess was cleaned up and the family later let me know that Jill's behavior was no longer a problem at school. This healing play demonstrates the power of puppets in the playroom.

Puppet-assisted play therapy occurs as a natural progression in the playroom. The children lead the way by playing with the puppets in any way they like. They work out their individual issues and concerns and heal via self-actualization.

When the therapist is on target and reflects the child's true accurate feelings, wishes and/or desires, the child will reassure the therapist that they are on the right track.

Since the child's communication in child-centered play therapy is in metaphor, it follows that the child's reactions to responses and reactions will also occur in metaphor. The child will continue with the play and may agree with the therapist's reflections. Another signal that illustrates a therapist is on the right track is when the child intensifies the play with more energy and excitement, e.g., louder or faster. If the therapist's reflections are accurate, they may play physically closer or invite the therapist to play.

If the therapist is off target, reactions will differ. The child will correct the therapist by saying "no," and sometimes explain verbally what they mean while still in metaphor. The child may change the play focus to another activity, demonstrate a loss of concentration, physically distance themself from the therapist, or stop the play completely. If the therapist is attuned to the child, they will know if they are on the right track and will be in harmony with the child (Norton & Norton, 1997).

To summarize, PAPT based on child-centered theory can successfully heal children. Child-centered therapy strives for self-actualization that is achieved through creative play, and creative play is enhanced via puppets; therefore, it follows that new experiences of self-actualization from puppet play are ideal.

Creativity goes hand in hand with puppets, innately producing new experiences. These new experiences provide for heightened self-actualization. The new experiences of self-actualization create new neural pathways. New neural pathways create neuroplasticity (our brains are plastic or moldable). What molds our brains? New experiences. Ergo, puppetry provides neuroplasticity, which in turn provides opportunities for change. Remember, when neurons fire together they wire together. This change, a new experience, leads to processing emotion using both parts of the brain together, creating integration, and integration allows for behavior regulation.

PAPT and Psychoanalytic Theory and Psychodynamic Theory

Psychoanalytic theory focuses on the psyche, unconscious, and dreams etc., while psychodynamic theory focuses on the human mind and personality as well but tries to broaden the understanding. Traditional psychoanalytic theory was originated by Sigmund Freud.

Psychodynamic theory refers to the ideas and perspectives that were derived from Freud's theory by his many followers. Carl Jung, Alfred Adler, Melanie Klein, John Bowlby, and Mary Ainsworth are just a few of the psychologists that contributed to this development. Although many different psychodynamic theories exist, they all emphasize unconscious motives and desires, as well as the importance of shaping childhood experiences.

Psychoanalytic theory rests on the idea that thought is largely influenced by irrational drives; these irrational drives are unconscious. Attempts to bring these drives into awareness or the consciousness meet resistance in the form of defense mechanisms. Conflicts between conscious and unconscious, or repressed material, create psychopathology. Healing is achieved through bringing this material into the conscious mind through skilled guidance or therapeutic intervention.

In psychodynamic theory, repressions also create psychopathology. All behavior is motivated by the expression of drives. In this theory, it is said that the personality develops out of *needs* to fulfill the pleasure principle.

Freud founded many important concepts. He specifically believed that the unconscious was important when understanding the human mind. He believed that all our fears and desires are restrained in the unconscious. Freud emphasized that, by making the unconscious thoughts known, healing can occur. He explained this through the components of id, ego, and superego. Id operates on the pleasure principle; superego operates on the morality principal. Ego moderates id and superego and tries to create a balance so that they satisfy the demands of id in a socially acceptable manner.

Psychodynamic theory also focuses on the inner conflict and the individual experiences and attempts to relieve this tension that the individual feels as a cure for the illness. Bringing the repressed emotions, behavior, etc., to the conscious so that the problem can be identified is the first step to this therapy

A child makes sense of their world through their play and play is a safe context to try out new things. During a puppet show in my playroom, a little girl whose mother had a newborn at home played out her wishes with a baby kangaroo puppet. She threw the baby out the "window" of the puppet stage. Not only was this cathartic for the little girl, her wishes of throwing the baby away were validated and hence brought into her consciousness, affording it expression. Most likely if her mother understood the context of this puppet play, she would have corrected this behavior of throwing the baby out. The issue in the child's puppet play was safely expressed and honored. Fantasy or content play communicates important information to the therapist about the issues. Non-content play can also communicate the child's feelings about the issue. The therapist can observe and interact while monitoring their own feelings during the interaction as well as the child's style. Is the child confident, resistant, proud, shameful, etc?

Superheroes fighting in puppet play may be an illustration of a struggle of repression of unconscious desire to assist a child with "playing out" conflicting perceptions. Various interpretations are possible. Perhaps this conflict can be used to identify who is their "hero" during their parents' high-conflict divorce.

It is not imperative to always be cognizant of the child's representations in order to be facilitative, but it is vital, if possible, to have ongoing consistent consultation with parents in order to proceed/succeed with the treatment progress.

Honoring this puppet play by validating feelings is an example of how PAPT has a role as a fundamental technique. The ultimate goal, as a child makes sense out of their world in play, is to recognize and understand the internal pressures of the child and remove impediments to normal development. Increasing the child's self-awareness and capacity for problem solving provides a re-set on a path to normal development for the child.

If invited, the play therapist may join the child in the puppet play, to enter into the child's fantasy life, supporting and encouraging by going along with the child's make believe.

The superheroes puppet show explored who was the hero, who was the victim, and who wins. Was the child portraying both of his heroes fighting? Perhaps exploring good versus evil? Or maybe the show represents the acceptance of the cause? Here, the play therapist helps the child explore the enactment, how it affects their feelings, thoughts, wishes, beliefs, and behaviors as they are played out.

Other possible interpretations of the superheroes conflict could be "playing with" goodness, i.e., mother. "Is my mother good? She hurts that which is bad, but is she good?" It could be an actual incident between the mother and father. Or perhaps it's wishing that one of the superheroes could come save them. Interpretations may not be crucial. What is important is that their puppet-assisted play therapy behavior is safer than actually throwing the infant out an actual window, or even punching/killing someone, or blowing up a house. It can provide resolution and create integration for the child.

"It is important not to verbalize interpretations of the material that the children reveal. If they bring it into reality, it is acceptable to join with them." Milton H. Erickson discovered that it is possible to resolve pain from trauma through these metaphors without knowing the content (Norton & Norton, 1997, p. 48). Because children play out their trauma, verbalizing details is not important to the child; however, understanding the situation and resolving the pain is. Children accomplish this work through their play.

PAPT and Object Relations Theory

Object relations theory is an offshoot or variation of psychoanalytic theory and emphasizes interpersonal relations, primarily in the family and especially between mother and child. This theory was developed by Melanie Klein, William Fairbairn, Anna Freud, Michael Balint, and Donald Winnincott. Object relations is based on the theory that the primary motivational factors in one's life are based on human relationships, rather than sexual or aggressive triggers, such as in Freud's theory. This suggests that the need for contact with others and to form relationships is our primary motivator. The focus is to pinpoint the difficulties in relationships with others and to modify them to help improve their interpersonal functioning.

In the context of object relations theory, the term "objects" refers not to inanimate entities but to significant others with whom an individual relates, usually one's mother, father, or primary caregiver. It is believed that infants form mental representations of themselves in relation to others and that these internal images significantly influence interpersonal relationships later in life. Since relationships are at the center of object relations theory, the person-therapist alliance is important to the success of therapy.

The term "object relations" refers to the dynamic internalized relationships between the self and significant others (objects). An object relation involves mental representations. The images do not necessarily reflect reality but are subjectively constructed by an infant's limited cognitive abilities (Good Therapy, n.d.a).

Puppets can be valuable tools in object relations therapy involving children. They can be the mental representation of their images. Sweeney and Homeyer (1999) explained that "the use of puppets as transitional objects serves as a developmental tool to allow children to bridge the gap between reality and fantasy...puppetry is developmentally appropriate for young children in therapy" (p. 268).

The term transitional object was coined in 1951 by Donald Winnicott as a term for any material object, typically something soft such as a blanket or stuffed toy, to which a child attributes a special value. The child makes a shift from the relationship with the mother to a genuine object relationship. The transitional object may be considered as a defense or antidote against separation anxiety. Puppet blankets are a perfect option.

PAPT and Jungian Theory

A central tenet in analytical psychology, which is Jung's term for his theory, is the ego–self axis. This concept refers to the nature of the relationship between the conscious (ego) and the unconscious mind (self). In healthy people there is a fluid yet regulated connection between the two zones. This complex theory addresses blocked or stuck emotions at the unconscious level. The focus is to integrate the psyche into a whole personality.

Puppets communicate by sharing unconscious material. Different types of puppets reveal the different archetypes that Jung referred to. Jung described archetypes as instincts coupled with images that direct and influence behavior and emotions. Archetypes are biological forces and drives in the unconscious that often transcend culture. They are found universally and bring a certain similarity to the human experience and understanding. They center around symbolic meanings of images such as birth, death, love, the great mother, the trickster, God,

Figure 4.1 Mom and Dad represented by the witch and dog

and the devil. John Allen suggested that much information can be gathered merely by observing the choice of puppets used (Sweeney & Homeyer, 1999).

Information can also be retrieved from a description of the images/ archetype. Bertoia shares an age-appropriate expression of death in this child's description of death within the "The Rosebush" projective technique. Oaklander's Rosebush Fantasy is further discussed in Chapter 7. "I look like a rosebush. I am a thorny rosebush. I have no flowers. My leaves are blood. My branches and stems are the color of guts. I have thorns that are as sharp as a razor blade. I am a mean bush" (Allan & Bertoia, as cited in Sweeney & Homeyer, 1999, p. 97).

O'Conner (2000) contended, "The nonverbal message is more accurate than the verbal" (p. 129). When examining the symbolic meaning or an archetype, it is clear what the connotation of the belief is that is being shared. A lion has a different message than a pussycat, and the sun has a different meaning than a rainstorm.

PAPT and Filial Therapy

Filial therapy is a child-centered therapy approach taught to parents and caregivers to assist children in both the playroom and at home. Mentioned earlier, nondirective play therapy or child-centered play therapy is based

Figure 4.2 Pizza night with new family members

on the humanistic theory. It helps parents deal with many situations that come up in everyday life with their children. Many techniques described in this book can fall under the term filial therapy because they are useful to parents. Puppet play is a great tool for parents seeking to learn how to communicate more effectively with their children. Puppet-assisted filial therapy involves inviting your puppet to join you and your family. PAPT gives parents additional tools to parent effectively.

In *Being a Brain-Wise Therapist*, Badenoch (2008) wrote, "When we can help parents understand that their relationship with their children is the most crucial factor in structuring a brain that can support self-regulation, warm relationships, and optimal learning, we have receptive ears" (p. 308). This is the premise of filial therapy.

My bear puppet, Bear-niece, joined our family when my daughter was young. Bear-niece was the "elder" of our home who assisted with communications in our household. She was the one who asked my daughter to come to dinner, to brush her teeth, to go to bed, and to clean her room. This approach resulted in easier compliance and more family fun.

The scientific basis for the effectiveness of using puppets to assist in play therapy is well established. PAPT contributes to children's growth, connections, healing, and fun. In the next two chapters we will plunge further into the practice of PAPT with detailed descriptions of techniques and interventions.

5   PAPT and Cognitive Behavioral Therapy

Therapists can use each theoretical platform with PAPT practice as an innate characteristic of their treatment. PAPT provides a basis for a relationship and environment in which the child can begin to heal. A child-friendly environment enables the cotherapist puppet to provide a feeling of safety by distance rather than face-to-face disclosure, enhancing these relationships. Puppets also facilitate work on children's other relational issues. The quickest and most effective way to achieve transformative moments with children is through the medium of play (Terr, 2008). Utilizing puppets in play makes these transformative moments occur faster and makes them more powerful. Puppets have the potential to catch children's attention even when they have difficulties focusing. They seem to reach the child at a very deep level.

The directive approach with the greatest amount of relevance to PAPT is cognitive behavioral therapy (CBT). One directive approach to CBT is called psychoeducation. The central concept of cognitive behavioral therapy is that most human emotion is the direct result of what people think, tell themselves, assume, or believe about themselves and their social situation. When people's beliefs, thoughts, and self-talk are rational, they feel emotions that are functional. When their beliefs, thoughts, and self-talk are disturbed or irrational, people develop dysfunctional emotions, affects, and behavior.

Cognitive behavioral therapy with children is based on teaching a child to change cognitive schemas that control their beliefs and perceptions as well as changing behavioral symptoms. Cognitive therapy is concerned with both how individuals perceive events and the cognitions based on these perceptions. The therapy focuses on symptom reduction and modification of attitudes, beliefs, and expectations. Cognitive behavior play therapy incorporates cognitive and behavioral interventions within a play therapy paradigm to change cognitive schemas (beliefs) as well as behaviors. "A therapist [or cotherapist puppet] can facilitate the child's cognitive reflection process, which identifies, challenges, and changes misconceptions, faulty beliefs, distorted cognitions, and irrational self-talk that have created dysfunctional emotions and behaviors" (Lantz, as cited in Turner, 1996, p. 100).

PAPT treatment can be communicated to children indirectly and puppets can be used to model the child's cognitive strategies such as maladaptive beliefs and then make positive self-statements to address the beliefs. Puppets can teach the errors of cognitive distortions that are prevalent in children who experience psychological distress or difficulties. Puppets are a dynamic medium used to teach therapeutic skills.

Most puppets can be used specifically for cognitive behavioral therapy. Teaching about CBT through the use of a three headed dragon can be effective for teaching this concept. Drews and Cavett (as cited in Drews & Schafer, 2018), explained,

> The use of three headed dragon puppet can visually show a child what we think, feel and do are interconnected. Cognitive behavior theory assumes that the way we think influences the way we feel and the way we feel has an impact on the way we act. In turn, the way we act can affect the way we think and the way we feel. Hence, what you think determines what you feel and that dictates what you do. The three-headed dragon can demonstrate this lesson. One head represents the dragon's thoughts, the second head his feelings,

Figure 5.1 CBT three-headed dragon puppet

and the third his behavior. The three components of the dragon are connected, and this connection portrays one's mental health. Awareness of this concept makes change possible.

(p. 156)

Many CBT techniques and skills can be taught to the children utilizing puppets. PAPT techniques include "learning to go into the shell," teaching about emotions, teaching mindsight and mindfulness, teaching about the brain, breathing techniques, imagery, role modeling, conflict resolution, teaching about the strengths perspective, bibliotherapy, and storytelling. Strengths perspective, bibliotherapy and storytelling again can also be used within additional theoretical approaches.

Figure 5.2 Can you go into your shell like Herman does?

To aid me in CBT, I created my own "cotherapist puppet" to work with me in my office, a master's level "So-Shell" worker named Herman the Turtle. Though Herman is a turtle, any animal chosen to accompany you will work. However, many of my interventions have evolved from Herman the Turtle. Therefore, numerous techniques in this book work best with a turtle.

Many therapists advise parents to teach children with angry feelings to stop, reflect, and take time to calm the body and mind. A favorite technique, "time in," is used as opposed to "time out." Time out seems to connote negativity and abandonment with directives to leave the area, go to your room, sit in the corner, etc. It is preferable to teach reflection as a positive skill rather than a punishment consequence. It allows the child to take some time for themselves, go inward, meditate, or stop and think. Similar to a turtle going into its shell, a child can have time in to redirect and get centered.

The skill depicted in this photo doesn't need to be taught. All children in my office reenact "going into their shell" the same way. Some behaviors are just universal.

Mindsight

Teaching "Mindsight" is another technique of cognitive behavioral therapy coined by Dan Siegel and Tina Bryson (2011) to describe our human capacity to perceive the mind of the self and others. It is a powerful lens through which we can understand our inner lives with more clarity, integrate the brain, and enhance our relationships with others. As these authors contended, learning about the mind helps develop it (Siegel & Bryson, 2011).

When we teach mindsight during cognitive behavioral therapy, we take moments of conflict and transform them into opportunities for learning, skill building, and brain development.

"This skill is used to teach the understanding of our own mind as well as understanding the mind of another. Mindsight is a kind of focused attention that allows us to see the internal workings of our own minds. It helps us get ourselves off of the autopilot of ingrained behaviors and habitual responses." It lets us "name and tame the emotions we are experiencing, rather than being overwhelmed by them" (Siegel & Bryson, 2011, pp. 105–110). The workings of our mind, or mindsight, are implemented by playing SIFT.

By teaching SIFT (Sensations, Images, Feelings, Thoughts) through the activity of our child's minds, we can help them recognize different "rim points" at work within and help them gain more insight and control in their lives. SIFTing helps us understand the important lesson that our bodily sensations shape our emotions, and our emotions shape our thinking as well as the images in our mind. Each of the "points on the rim" (sensations, images, feelings and thoughts) can influence the others and together they create our state of mind.

(Siegel & Bryson, 2011, pp. 105–110)

To play the SIFT game in PAPT, a therapist uses both their and the child's puppets to teach by asking questions that aid the SIFT process, specifically about a child's sensations, images, feelings, and thoughts. *Mention* something about the *sensations* of the puppet's body while they experience the information related to the questions asked. *Inquire* about the child's puppet's possible *sensations*. *Inquire* about the child's own sensations of being in the playroom. Is the puppet hungry? What does that feel like in your body when you are hungry? Ask what *images* are going through the mind of the child's puppet. For example, Herman has an image of himself with his turtle friends swimming in the ocean. Question the child or their puppet about how Herman is *feeling* while he is swimming with his friends. Is he happy and excited? Often children need assistance at the beginning of this game and require a list of possible options or suggestions for possible feeling states. What are the child's *thoughts*? Are they or their puppet thinking about playing a new game? The SIFT game is appropriate in the midst of any play activity.

In the SIFT game, the particular puppet used dictates the imagery the child is experiencing. For example, if you use a puppy puppet in the SIFT game, the puppet can feel the *sensations* of the weather on its fur, how it feels when the owner scratches it's head, the grass on its back as it rolls in a field, or the coolness of the river when it jumps in to swim. Puppies might *imagine* their owner picking up a leash when it is time for a walk, reaching in the cookie jar for a doggie treat, or chasing a cat down the street. Puppies have *feelings* too. They get lonely when they are in the house by themselves, feel loved when they are petted, feel hungry when it is dinner time, or feel sad when they lose a dog companion. *Thoughts* are incorporated in this exercise. A puppy can think of wanting to go for a walk or what to do for his next treat.

Different perspectives can certainly change a person's thoughts, feelings, behaviors, and sensations. An example of a perspective change occurred in my office when I asked a child if he could be any animal he wanted, which puppet would he choose? He said he would like to be the deer in the woods (he hunted with his father). I asked him about the sensations and the images he would have if he were that deer and he shared his projected images and sensations. I asked what he would be feeling, and he said scared. He continued, "The deer would be scared of getting shot in the woods and would think, *oh no*. I wish no one would shoot me." Interestingly enough, I later learned that due to this SIFT game using the perspective of the deer, this child no longer wanted to go hunting.

Siegel and Bryson (2011) discussed mindfulness as it pertains to mindsight. As mindsight is a kind of focused attention that allows us to see the internal workings of our own minds, mindfulness involves consciously bringing awareness to the here and now experience with openness, curiosity and flexibility. Kabat-Zinn (as cited in Harris, n.d.) defined mindfulness as being present in the here and now, living in the moment, being aware of what is around you without judgment. Mindfulness reminders are used in PAPT while children are engrossed playing with the puppets. For example, observe that angry puppet and describe what the puppet does next.

PAPT can be valuable in mindfulness exercises. Siegel and Bryson (2011) contend that just talking about the mind helps you develop it. To introduce teaching about the mind, I created Bryan, the brain puppet (Figure 5.3). I use Bryan the Brain to assist with the science and brain explanations while working with children. PAPT addresses CBT by teaching about the brain so that children may understand the notion of change.

Dan Siegal and other neurobiologists claim that the more one knows about the brain the more one is able to understand themself and the world around them. Children begin to feel more hopeful about their situation when they learn about neuroplasticity and how their brains can change. Teaching children what is happening in their brain when they feel themselves losing control is an effective strategy for helping them avoid "flipping their lid," a term that Siegel and Bryson (2011) coined for when control is lost.

My puppet, Bryan the Brain (or Bryanna the Brain), can help with this. Bryan and Bryanna are cute, engaging, and charming puppets.

Why is it important to teach about the brain, mindfulness, and being in the present? Mindfulness is a concept that has become a popular phenomenon to help patients become grounded or stay in the "window of tolerance." The "window of tolerance" is a term coined by Dr. Siegel used to describe the zone of arousal in which a person is able to function most effectively. When people are within this zone, they are typically able to readily receive, process, and integrate information and otherwise respond to the demands of everyday life without much difficulty (Siegel, 1999).

Extending beyond the window of tolerance, when a threat to survival occurs, either physically or mentally, most people react using either fight, flight, or freeze mode. When this is activated, it is said that the

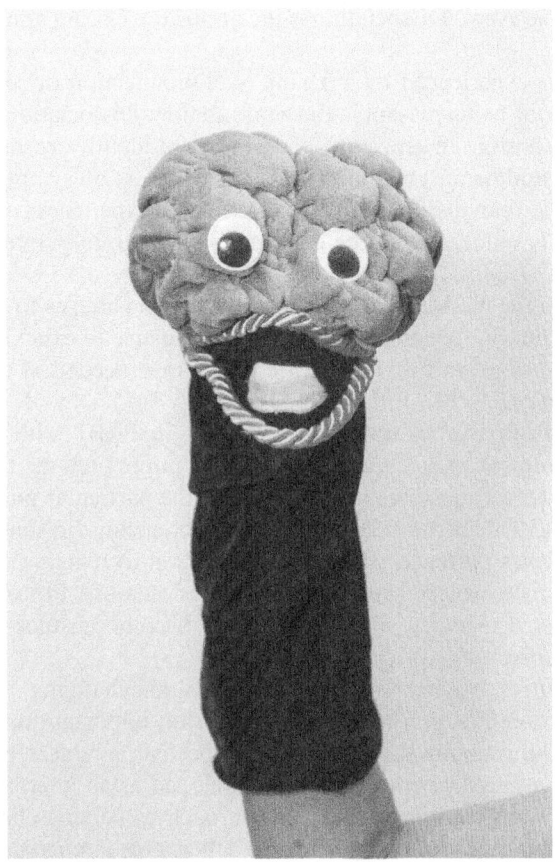

Figure 5.3 Bryan the Brain puppet (Bryan the Brain is available for purchase at
www.ferniecounselling.ca)

lower or reptilian brain hijacks the upper brain and the person is not
thinking or behaving with focused attention.

When a person is within their window of tolerance, the brain is
functioning well and can effectively process stimuli. The person is likely
to be able to reflect, think rationally, and make decisions calmly without
feeling either overwhelmed or withdrawn (GoodTherapy, n.d.b).

Learning how to stay in the window of tolerance or to expand
your own personal window of tolerance via focusing helps mitigate
or stop dissociation tendencies. Although dissociation is the first line
of defense for children who experience scary, painful, or traumatic

events, it is problematic when dissociation becomes automatic during any uncomfortable event. Dissociation is the opposite of being mindful or present.

Dissociation is experienced by a feeling of disconnection or separation from a state of being present in the here and now. Dissociation can be defined as disruptions in aspects of consciousness, identity, memory, physical actions, and/or the environment. When dissociation symptoms become severe, they can disrupt daily life. Dissociated experiences make people continually vulnerable to the emergence of disruptive states of mind (Badenoch, 2008).

Mindfulness is the method of changing dissociative patterns to help children stay in the window of tolerance, so they are able to experience the present, process memories, and create the change needed in their lives to help them reach their full potential.

Interruption from dissociation can be taught in PAPT with any puppet. The therapist can ask a child, "Can your puppet tell me three sounds, three textures, and three smells?" Again, the particular puppet that you are using dictates the imagery you are experiencing. To sum up, mindfulness achieves presence, which allows children to remain in the window of tolerance, which is required to process memory. Processed memory or digested memory allows children to become unstuck and attains optimal functioning of each child.

Because cognitive behavioral therapy focuses on changing one's perspective, the strengths perspective principle is an important aspect of change. Teaching about the strengths perspective enhances positive change. The strengths perspective was developed as an alternative to the more common pathology-oriented approach to helping clients. Instead of focusing on client's problems and deficits, the strengths perspective identifies and elicits the client's strengths and assets in assisting them with their problems and goals (Compton & Galaway, 1999).

A technique used to teach and build the skill of utilizing the strengths perspective is to identify a puppet's strengths. Acknowledging strengths can change perspectives for the better. Have a child choose an animal puppet and encourage them to make a list of how the chosen animal behaves. For example, "Is the canine a guard dog or a puppy puppet?" This will assist the therapist (or cotherapist puppet) in determining how that animal can be used therapeutically in their situation. Have the child imagine what they would consider the positive attributes of the animal puppet (make a list). What would the animal puppet's short comings be? (Make a list.) Help the child with additional ideas by mentioning advantages and shortcomings. Ask them what the best ways would be to overcome the animal's limitations. This exercise is an example of working with the strengths perspective.

Additional CBT Strategies

One of my favorite books, *The Enchanted Tree* by Flavia and Lisa Weedn (1995), illustrates the strengths perspective. PAPT utilizes this book with a Tree Puppet (available at www.ferniecounselling.ca). In my playroom, Herman the Turtle tells a story, adapted from a turtle in this book. The story he tells is that one day, this turtle came to see him. She was very unhappy because she had a *turtle hurdle*. She was a small turtle and moved very slowly. She wanted to be like the big turtles where she lived. They were much larger than her and moved much quicker. Herman asked the turtle what she thought the advantages might be of her small size and she said that since she was slower and closer to the ground she could see crickets and all the other amazing bugs that were also close to her on the ground. She said she was the first to see the tiny budding spring flowers that came up after the rain. Then the little turtle realized that there were advantages to being small instead of being big like the other turtles. She realized that it was okay to be different and be who she was. She said that she now understood that we are all special in our own wonderful way. She decided that she liked how and who she was and was happy and grateful about being small. She sang and danced as she left the office.

Another crucial component of CBT is the use of proper breathing techniques. One way to describe this concept to the child is comparing it to an ambulance call. For example, on almost every call the paramedics will give oxygen to the patient. We discuss how when our physical body is in shock, our system needs oxygen. Similarly, psychological stress needs it as well. Through breathing exercises, you can learn to minimize stress reactions. Additional oxygen is necessary to function well in stressful situations. Breathing exercises are important to master.

One PAPT breathing exercise is to have a puppet bend in half (from the wrist) and raise up again while inhaling. We dialogue about how breathing is an important aspect of body awareness. I say: "When you are frightened, nervous, or excited your breathing becomes shallow and fast. You need to breathe deeper and slower." We experiment with our puppet friend until the child understands.

Another hands-on technique is to ask the child to pretend that he and his puppet are helping to blow up a balloon. As the balloon is deflating, have both the child and the puppet bend over or fall in half. As the balloon is inflating, raise up or stand up. Do this exercise three times.

Blowing bubbles is a favorite breathing technique for children. Puppets love to watch bubble blowing competitions.

Another important therapy technique within the framework of CBT is imagery. Imagery is a skill taught to assist children with various issues they find challenging when they need comforting. Whether a child needs additional calming or forcefulness, they can acquire this by achieving a mindset from their imagination. Any fantasy can be used to contact the wise and creative spirit of a child.

PAPT is a preferred method for teaching additional CBT techniques and skills. Role playing for problem solving is one technique. In Saenz's (2002) book *Powerful Puppetry*, role plays using puppets are presented for numerous situations that may cause distress. One example of resolving conflict resolution is to have two classmates fighting on the playground. The child chooses two puppets to represent the classmates. The puppets decide if the disagreement is important and really worth fighting over (apparently it is), they investigate and find out how each puppet feels, they negotiate and find a way to give both puppets what they want (such as a compromise to their argument). If the puppets can't resolve the conflict it is suggested by one puppet to seek adult help.

Puppets are quite competent as tools for conflict resolution and problem-solving ideas for diverse issues. Other topics cited in *Powerful Puppetry* are related to family relationships, caring, cooperation, happiness, self-esteem, fairness, citizenship, respect, safe behavior, and anger management (Saenz, 2002). During a role modeling puppet show, the therapist's puppet may ask the child "What do I say (or do) now?" This model demonstrates ways to experiment with problem solving that can be helpful with the therapeutic process.

All the numerous methodologies used to help teach conflict resolution to a child can be taught using puppets. For example, a brother and sister are watching television and the sister wants the channel changed. A fight ensues. Your puppets "show" the siblings how to resolve a conflict instead of punching each other or irritating each other.

One PAPT-adapted technique from Mattise in relation to problem solving is called "On the one hand... and then the other" (Kaduson & Schaefer, 1997). "On the one hand" and "and then the other" are the names of two puppets that are presented as having conflicting ideas and feelings. The puppets may be used to teach children how to identify and assimilate conflicting feelings surrounding a problem. Puppets can pose questions to each other that correspond to the child's dilemma. The puppets can agree, disagree, or agree to disagree. They can express contradictory feelings about the same event or experience or address conflicting feelings that may surface in the threats of suicide, alcoholism, divorce, and sexual abuse. This technique brings attention to the push/pull feelings that may occur.

Mattise offers processing questions such as, "What kinds of different feelings might we feel at the same time?," "What can we do if these feelings are very strong?," "What can we do if we are feeling confused about these feelings?," "What can we do if thinking or worrying about these feelings takes lots of our time, attention and/or energy?," and "What can we do if these feelings leave us feeling sad or mad most of the time?" (Kaduson & Schaefer, 1997).

A puppet show can also be used as a role modeling technique in CBT to teach children a behavior or a success by providing an example of the preferred values, attitudes, and behaviors associated with a role.

Puppets also allow children the opportunity to try on different social roles and other forms of interpersonal communication. When we role play a particular character, we bring ourselves and our own experiences into the playing out of that character. Role playing assists with developing a more positive self-concept. For example, two puppets can present a puppet show with a plan detailing what to do in case of an emergency, such as calling 911 for help. The puppets can be calm, and possibly responsible for pets. Herman has a *shell phone* that we use for practice.

Role modeling with puppets can be used for numerous teachings. These include several of the facets of mindsight, assertiveness, empathetic responses, active listening, accountability, interviewing, and creative problem solving. These skills may be role modeled by the cotherapist puppet or by putting on a puppet show. One child used the great wise old owl puppet to be the creative problem solver in his puppet show. The owl had some very helpful ideas. One of the ideas was to talk to his teacher. His owl saved the day.

Puppet storytelling can be used to teach consequences and identify feelings to assist with conflict resolution. In the projective storytelling strategies, asking the puppet what they can do about a situation can illicit some very creative problem solving. Cotherapist puppet can ask questions such as: "I wonder, Mr. Mouse, how it feels when you are chased and bullied by the cat?" All the numerous methodologies used to help teach conflict resolution to a child can be taught using puppets.

Storytelling is another technique intrinsic to CBT. Clinicians have had impressive success with storytelling. Sources for stories include movies, cartoon themes, fairy tales, books, and the imagination of the child or therapist. Storytelling is nonconfrontational and does not directly address the child's symptoms. When using this technique, it is important to know something about the child and their life and to quickly understand the main themes of their story. Themes can be statements like: "It is ok to love the Daddy tiger but not like the bad/ mean stuff he does to the baby tiger," or "That little mouse got bullied by the cat and now he is upset and taking it out on her mice friends. What do you think?" Children can incorporate the stories to restructure their thought processes and attitudes towards their issues. Puppets can be used to help children recognize, identify, and begin to cope with difficulties that create conflicting emotions within them.

With storytelling, solutions are presented in a metaphorical manner that is used to help children resolve conflicts and problems. The unique nature of a metaphor is that it allows the information to bypass the conscious level and enter into the child's unconscious. Metaphors help children make sense of the new experiences. Metaphors allow children to use their imagination and help make sense of new experiences. These reparative experiences and the child's imagination are the premise for change and healing. Mills and Crowley (1986) asserted that the metaphors of the story activate the child's imagination, allowing healing through strength, self-knowledge, and transformation.

Siegel and Bryson (2011) contended that "storytelling is a powerful activity for integrating implicit and explicit memory" (p. 79). Therapists can create stories with a hero or protagonist who owns similar difficulties but overcomes them by learning new skills (Mills & Crowley, 1986). The ends of the stories are positive and successful as in the animal strengths perspective exercise mentioned earlier.

Mills and Crowley (1986) offered several basic ingredients of story making to create a metaphorical storyline with your puppet, including:

1. Presenting a metaphorical conflict similar to that of the child's conflict.
2. Personifying unconscious processes via various characters such as heroes and villains, which represent the potentials and fears of the protagonist.
3. Integrating parallel learning situations that result in the protagonist's victory and success.
4. Presenting a metaphorical crisis that eventually becomes a turning point in the resolution of conflict.
5. Developing a new sense of identity for the protagonist since his victory.
6. Culminating this resolution into a celebration and sense of new identity.

Nancy Davis's (1966) comprehensive book titled *Therapeutic Stories to Teach and Heal* provides stories needed for most individualized treatment plans that can be used with puppets.

In summary, cognitive behavioral therapy is a popular, highly researched, directive therapy that addresses change through the theoretical platform of cognitive behavior theory. The different techniques of CBT are intertwined into numerous therapeutic treatment modalities that easily fit into puppet-assisted play therapy.

6   PAPT and Other Theories

PAPT addresses significant issues that can be presented dramatically in simple scenes, and the metaphorical messages are quite powerful. They seem to reach the child at a very deep level.

The psychology of the therapist has a lot to do with the choice of method used. The particular school of thought followed by different therapists (Freud, Young, Adler, etc.) is the basis of the theoretical model used for treatment by each individual therapist. The therapist's approach to puppetry, the way puppets are introduced to the child, and even the particular characterization of the puppets may all influence the various therapeutic techniques implemented. It is interesting to compare these theories with therapeutic techniques.

In this chapter we will discuss using PAPT with systems theory, filial therapy, attachment theory represented by Theraplay and developmental therapy, Adlerian theory and Adlerian therapy, and solution-focused therapy, which is based on numerous theories. PAPT techniques are effective with each one of these theoretical platforms and approaches.

Kevin O'Conner, the author of the *Play Therapy Primer: An Integration of Theories and Techniques* (2000), stated that the same approaches and techniques can be used with different theoretical bases (Personal communication, July 16, 2014). In short, PAPT techniques often stay the same, although the theoretical platforms may differ.

For example, using puppets in storytelling can be a valuable tool across the whole spectrum of theories. O'Connor explains that storytelling can be psychoeducational if coming from the theoretical perspective of cognitive behavior theory. If you teach social skills, storytelling can be avenues of expression with insight focus related to psychodynamic theory. If a puppet from the family reads a story with a caregiver, attachment theory is the foundation for the treatment to gain a more secure attachment. If storytelling is incorporated into the miracle question such as; "If a miracle occurred what would your day be like?", it follows that solution-focused therapy, as pioneered by Shazer in 1978, is the basis for treatment. How a therapist uses each intervention will depend on its fit with the different theories.

The puppet is an intrinsic element of these therapies. The cotherapist puppet is a member of the healing team. Children find it easier to engage with a puppet because the therapist is not talking directly to the child. Refraction, a term used to describe a threesome in this therapy scenario, helps implicit memories become explicit memories (explained in Chapter 2). When the memories become explicit they become full of meaning, thus they don't have such hidden power.

While utilizing any of these theories with puppets in the playroom, classroom, or at home, refraction is implemented by talking directly to the cotherapist puppet about the child. Try wondering out loud with your puppet. Talk to the puppet and ask about the child, "I am wondering if Johnny understands…?" Paraphrase with your puppet. "Johnny seems to think…" Summarize with your puppet, "I think I heard Johnny say…" Check in with your puppet, "How do you think Johnny is doing?"

These methods of refraction will allow for more comprehensive understanding and connection with the children with whom you work.

PAPT and Systems Theory

Systems theory is based on the family at large and their influence on the child.

The premise of systems theory is that all parts of any system are interrelated, interconnected, and interdependent. These systems are referring to the child's family system(s), and therefore it is imperative when evaluating a child's functioning to take into account the influence of their culture, traditions, multi-generational issues, and the families' and caregivers' influences in their life. This is especially obvious when dysfunctional families preclude their influence on the situation and drop the child off to be fixed.

Every child grows up in a complex structure which profoundly affects them. Each family member also engages in different roles within a family system that can change depending on the family dynamics at the time or external circumstances. The family itself is profoundly affected as well, as it is governed by its rules and different roles. Learning these structures helps us obtain information about the family system. Rules and values within these family systems are so ingrained that they dominate the basic foundation of the family. These ingrained rules are ever present during puppet play with families. This information is invaluable for the treatment plan.

This concept of the ingrained structure of the family was illustrated in a play therapy slide presentation by Liana Lowenstein (2002) at the

Association of Play Therapy Conference. The modality was sand tray therapy. The children were asked to build a sand tray with no rules. One of the children placed a policeman figurine in the tray and when asked the significance of the figurine chosen and placement, the child explained that the figurine was needed so that no one could make any rules. Though this child did not want to comply with the rules of the family, the idea of no rules was an incomprehensible situation due to the family dynamics of limit setting. Who is making the rules or script of the puppet show, who has the leading role, if any, etc?

When working with systems theory, it may be obvious at times that a child is merely a scapegoat or IP (identified patient) in a chaotic or malfunctioning family (D. Ingram, personal communication, 2010). The fact that a child has been singled out as the problem in the family system, and has done something to call attention to themselves, by alerting external systems, indicates that the child needs support. From a **systems** perspective, it is beneficial to see the child initially in a family session to witness the family dynamics play out. Then use individual sessions if the family is too dysregulated to support the child during discovery and transition. Individual puppet play can illustrate how the child's family is affecting them both for the therapist as well as the child.

Puppet play helps children achieve a closer understanding of themselves by giving them permission to go outside of themselves. In puppet play, children never really leave themselves, they just use more of themselves in the improvisational experience as they invent scenarios. The unconscious mind and the shut down parts of themselves surface. The puppet show itself is a vehicle for self-awareness.

For example, with divorce it appears to be a common dynamic for children to keep their feelings well-hidden because they don't want to cause their parents any more grief or pain. This may or may not be hidden from their own awareness. Children who have been victimized in other capacities may also experience feelings of protection for their parents. These protective feelings often emerge during family puppet play, i.e., puppets are victims being torn by two possible perpetrators. Oaklander (1978) described this new awareness as follows:

> The drama becomes a natural tool to help them [children] find and give expression to lost and hidden parts of themselves, and to build strength and selfhood.
>
> In creative dramatics, children learn about the world around them as they experience their re-enactments of their lives combined with their fantasy and imagination.
>
> We play out the parts in our own dreams, we create scenes, we rewrite as we go along. We don't just talk about the pain in our

chest, we give voice to it. Become it. We play out our mother, ourselves as children, our critical side, and so forth. We find that as we play these parts, we become more aware of ourselves, more involved, more real. We can allow suppressed parts of ourselves to emerge. We can let ourselves experience absorption, excitement, and spontaneity that may be lacking in our day-to-day lives.

(p. 139)

Directed puppet play can also enhance creativity. Ask questions that encourage children to stretch their imagination. Your creativity may enable issues to surface and open up opportunities to be addressed within the family system. Children display their needs, wants, and desires with the puppets in these shows.

An example of creating is to have a puppet show with a puppet on each hand of the client. Instruct the child to have their puppets face each other, and one puppet relates something difficult to the other puppet that may recently have happened to the child. Each storyline needs a beginning, middle, and end. Share how this difficulty felt. Have the other puppet help process the difficulty or validate to the original puppet having the struggle.

Another strategy used in systems theory, to learn about the family systems, is a genogram. A genogram is a family tree that maps out the history of the family and uses special symbols to describe relationships, major events, and the dynamics of the family over multiple generations. Many therapists do genograms on paper and others create a genogram in the sand tray. Puppets also can be valuable tools for a genogram. I have labeled these genograms puppet-o-grams.

This picture of a geno-puppet-o-gram (Figure 6.1) displays a person's family relationships and history. It goes beyond a traditional family tree. A puppet or puppets represents each pattern, pattern of behavior, and relationship. Repetitive patterns of behavior can be identified by visually tracking the familiar tendencies. Patterns of neglect, domestic violence, physical and sexual abuse, rigid rules, etc., can all be tracked in a genogram.

PAPT puppet-o-grams incorporate puppet play with the traditional genogram. The puppet-o-gram can be used as an assessment tool with family members as well as the extended family. Have a child choose a puppet that best reflects their thoughts and feelings about each family member. One puppet should represent the child. An option is to have the child make their own puppet in session as a new character. This may be additional assessment information. Children are asked to use any puppet and not limit themselves to people puppets. The type of puppet (people, animal, or object) chosen adds insight for the therapist as to

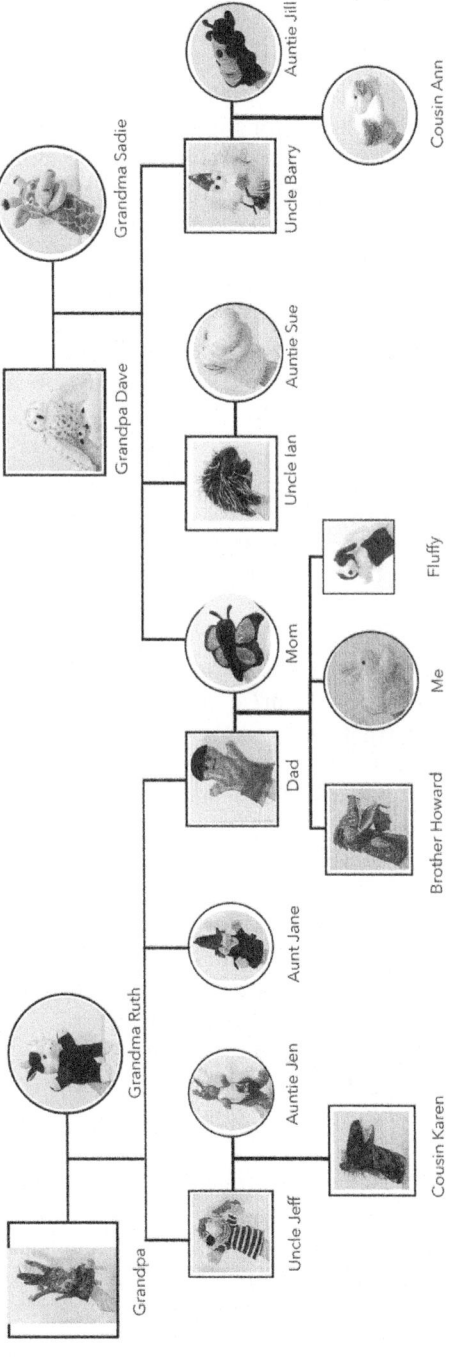

Figure 6.1 Geno-puppet-o-gram

the need to make things once removed. The choice of an aggressive dinosaur puppet is equally telling when chosen to represent someone in the family.

Children may choose to use multiple puppets to represent one person, for example, a clown and bunny for a sibling. In my playroom, I witnessed eye-opening information with this exercise. I had a mother represented by an aggressive dinosaur and the father by a snail. This information is a powerful communication tool to learn about clients and their families.

When symbols or metaphoric language are used with puppets, children and/or families go beyond what is already acknowledged or understood cognitively. They tap into their unconscious mind, which may provide the foundations for future understanding and problem solving. PAPT is a metaphoric medium and can serve as the language of the family system.

PAPT and Solution-Focused Therapy

Solution-focused therapy is a therapy model of how people change and how to interact with them as a client. Turner's model addresses three questions:

1. What is the cause of the present problem?
2. What maintains the problem?
3. How do we construct solutions?

Solution-focused therapy is not just a technique but a model of therapy that guides the resolution process as opposed to a theoretical platform. The principals of this therapy are:

1. An empirical orientation is supported. Speculative theorizing about the client's problems and behaviors is avoided.
2. This model approach is focused on problem solving.
3. The focus of treatment is on a specific problem.
4. Problems occur in the context of multiple systems. Contextual language may be needed.
5. Short term.
6. Collaborative.
7. An intervention with a well-defined sequence of activities.

The change is brought about primarily through problem-solving actions or tasks taken by the client/child within and outside the session (Turner, 1996).

This therapy consists of Shazer's miracle question, or the magic question, to help formulate goals. The therapist asks, "If a miracle happened tonight and you wake up tomorrow with the problem solved, or at least you thought you were on the right track to solving it, what would you be *doing* differently?"

The value of PAPT in solution-focused therapy is noteworthy. In my office I use a Genie in a Lamp puppet that asks the child to make one magic wish. I was informed by one child that I was wrong. When I asked him why, he said he had three wishes – not just one! This seems to be a great example of starting where the client is while utilizing puppets.

Figure 6.2 You have three wishes from your magic Genie

PAPT and Attachment Theory

In the field of play therapy attachment theory has become a very important foundational, heavily researched concept. Most play therapy modalities, such as Theraplay, filial therapy, child-centered, etc., include attachment or the importance of a relationship as one of the core beliefs. The neurobiology of attachment has taken off with the advancement in science and experts such as Dr. Bruce Perry, Paris Goodyear-Brown, and Dr. Karyn Purvis to name a few. British psychologist John Bowlby (1988) was the first attachment theorist, describing attachment as a lasting psychological connectedness between human beings. Attachment theory is focused on the relationships and bonds between people, particularly long-term relationships, including those between a parent and child and between romantic partners.

PAPT is capable of greatly enhancing relationship attachments. Attachment is a theory developed by psychologists to explain how a child interacts with the adults looking after them. If a child has a healthy attachment, this means the child can be confident that the adults will respond with reassurance and comfort to the child's needs if they are hungry, tired, or frightened (Child Protection Resource, n.d.).

> The attachment theory hypothesizes that the caregiver is instrumental during the first few years of a child's life. During this time, the child develops an internal working model of themselves in relation to their caregiver. Working models are internal representations that develop through daily interactions with a caregiver. These interactions form the child's expectations of how he/she will be treated. These models can predict other's behaviors hence, become self-fulfilling prophesies constant over time.
>
> (Bowlby, 1988)

Theraplay is a modality that focuses on the attachment theory. Theraplay speaks to the attachment theory premise that there is a fundamental need for a healthy early relationship. Theraplay is an approach based on the idea that parents can improve their children's behavior and also help them overcome emotional problems by engaging with their children with attunement and empathy. Studies have shown that Theraplay is effective in improving the parent–child relationship through play and healthy interaction.

Theraplay interactions focus on four essential qualities found in parent–child relationships: structure, engagement, nurture, and challenge. Theraplay treatment focuses on guiding the parent and child through playful nurturing. It helps the child feel secure, cared for, connected, and worthy. Theraplay is an ideal partner with PAPT. Introducing a parent puppet as a caregiver to the child reinforces the secure attachment necessary for a healthy and nurturing relationship.

PAPT and Developmental Play Therapy

There is a growing body of research that outlines the positive impact of healthy physical contact on people of all ages. Barnard and Brazelton (1990) found that loving touch produces oxytocin and releases endogenous opioids, which are known to solidify mother–infant bonds. It is important that all children experience gentle, kind, loving, and safe touch. Many studies have found that withholding touch is as damaging as inappropriate touch. This can be illustrated with children from orphanages who struggle with attachments.

It is accepted that touch is an important modality for creating relationships. Touch communicates safety, acceptance, playfulness, and empathy. Touch also helps regulate a child's out-of-sync emotions. A hug will calm an upset child.

In the playrooms as well as classrooms of today, touch has become an ethical dilemma. Does one hug or not hug? Sexually abused children are generally uncomfortable being touched or sexually act out with those who show them any type of healthy affection. Adults in many environments are prohibited to hug due to the sexual nature or connotation of this touch. The ethical issues will be examined later in this book.

PAPT can engage the use of hugs while avoiding the ethical questions and can help foster attachment. "Hugs are crucial for children. They help the immune system, cure depression, induce sleep, reduce stress, are rejuvenating, have no unpleasant side effects, are free, are non-fattening" (Sparks, 1993, p. 15). When you work with children, practice hugging your puppet and have your puppet hug the children you work with. Touch utilizing puppets will expedite the development of a secure attachment with the children.

PAPT and Adlerian Theory

The compatibility of Adlerian theory and PAPT is perfect as the use of puppets and Adlerian play therapy are an exceptional combination. According to Adlerian theory, the following issues are essential in the formation of each individual's personality:

1. People have a need to belong;
2. People move toward goals;
3. People are creative and unique; and

4. People experience life from a subjective perspective (Adler, 1927, as cited in Kottman & Meany-Walen, 2016).

Social interest, which describes a sense of social connectedness and a person's concern and actions that work toward the betterment of society, is another important concept in Adlerian theory. Adler believed that people were born with the capacity for social interest, but it had to be taught and fostered by adults in a child's life. A person's social interest is a measurement of their mental health (Sweeney, 2009). In observing children at play, we can see their whole attitude towards life. Play is of the utmost importance to every child (Adler, 1927, as cited in Kottman and Meany-Walen, 2016). Adlerian play therapy consists of four phases:

1. Building an egalitarian relationship with the child;
2. Investigating the child's lifestyle;
3. Gaining insight into the child's lifestyle; and
4. Reorienting /reeducating (Stutey et al., 2017).

Each of these phases is conducive to PAPT because the premise is that each person has a need to belong and gain significance.

It follows then that people join clubs to feel a sense of belonging. In my office, Herman created a "Turtle Club." It is an all-inclusive club. The only requirement to belong to the Turtle Club is to like Herman. Using Herman and his club absolutely helps to create a sense of belonging. Children who are club members create turtle art, bring turtle photos to sessions, construct clay turtles, and sing turtle songs. One child even had a turtle tattoo stamped on her leg. They become immersed with Herman, Herman's House, what Herman says, what he does, and how he feels.

PAPT and Ego State Theory

Gordon Emmerson, Ph.D., describes ego state theory as a powerful and brief therapy based on the premise that personality is composed of separate parts, rather than being a homogeneous whole. These parts, which everyone has, are called ego states. The therapist learns to work directly with the state that can best benefit from change, rather than merely working with an intellectual, talkative state.

We are each made up of a number of different ego states or parts; each has its own feelings, attributes, and accomplishments. The ego states are emotions, logic, skills, and other personal traits. When we say, "Part of me wants to...," we are talking about an ego state. When we say, "I feel at peace with myself on this issue," we are talking about our ego states agreeing, not having an internal struggle e.g.: a procrastin- ator part and leader part. Ego state therapy focuses on understanding and accepting each part with compassion. When two ego states are in conflict, we may feel torn on an issue or a decision (Ego State Therapy International, n.d.).

Working with ego states fits well with PAPT. The PAPT technique that pertains to ego state theory is called *Moo-Baa-Neigh*. Each animal puppet can represent the different ego states or parts of us that we iden- tify with e.g., a calm fish, a scaredy cat, or a ferocious lion. This activity enhances understanding and healing. A detailed explanation of how to utilize *Moo-Baa-Neigh* can be found in Chapter 14.

In summary, all theoretical platforms are an excellent fit for puppet- assisted play therapy. Caregivers report that children love coming into play therapy and are interested in their therapeutic pursuits. It is getting them to leave Herman's House (my office) that is the most difficult.

7   PAPT and the Four Stages of Therapy

The four basic components of practice process are engagement, assessment, intervention, and evaluation. PAPT techniques and interventions are effective in all of them. Keep in mind certain PAPT techniques can often address two or more of the basic components at the same time, so the boundaries between the four components can overlap. This is especially true of assessment, which occurs continuously throughout the process.

The sky is the limit when it comes to puppetry techniques and therapists can transform their practice by utilizing puppets. With puppets, you can implement adaptations from authors, interventions, and art that have been used with success. Puppets help therapists explore new ways to free their own creative spirit.

A good start to implementing PAPT is to challenge resistance to creative thinking that at first might seem impractical and unrealistic. Byron Norton stated in one of his trainings that "If you feel silly doing it [intervention], you are on the right track" (Norton & Norton, 1997). The airlines advise passengers to put on their own oxygen masks before helping their child. A similar rule holds true for creativity and PAPT. A therapist must enhance their own creativity before working with a child's. Several books are available on the subject of creativity. I recommend *Loosen Up* by Rasmussen and Rasmussen (1997) and *Make Your Creative Dreams Real* by SARK (2004).

My Herman the Turtle puppet is a theme used as much as possible in my office. He appears to be loved by all my clients. If PAPT had a motto, it might be "Two heads are better than one."

Although Herman is incorporated into most scenarios, the creation of other themes are effective as well. One child loved superheroes, so Herman became Super Turtle with the addition of a red cape. As I mentioned before, the sky is the limit when it comes to creativity and puppetry techniques.

Figure 7.1 Herman and me

Theme play creates enthusiasm in children and creates a continuous narrative for the client. Most themes work; however, it is important to be sensitive to the child's culture, traditions, and family systems. It is a personal preference to use a turtle because I fell in love with Herman's eyes. I learned later that in some Native traditions, a turtle represents healing and protection. I use Herman as a theme in my playroom and have adjusted and adapted many other ideas to fit Herman. I incorporate my techniques and interventions to be "Hermanized."

Any puppets in a playroom can dictate themes for therapy. Once a therapist has chosen a primary "cotherapist puppet" more adaptations can be used to implement the theme, from creating the puppet's own logo to collecting assorted themed supplies. For example, I created *Herman's Be Better Bubbles*. I attach homemade labels to generic bubble bottles that are purchased at a local store. I explain to the child that Herman blows bubbles in the sea where he swims when he is stressed. I ask a child, "Can you?"

Bubbles used to teach breathing techniques are a very effective intervention in play therapy. The slower you blow, the bigger the bubbles. The slower and deeper the breaths, the more therapeutic is the exercise.

A contest with members of a child's family to see who can blow the biggest bubbles in session works well. "Homework" can be assigned to practice bubble blowing at home. I recommend keeping the bubble bottle on the kitchen table at home to redirect stressful situations when they arise.

To enhance your puppet(s) theme, animal themed toys are everywhere. You can find them at arts and craft stores, thrift stores, garage sales, flea markets, online, quarter machines at gas stations, the dollar store, as candy, or even erasers. Then your cotherapist puppet animal is present whenever you work with a child.

Caregivers have informed me that the children call my office "Herman's House." This therapeutic alliance creates a lasting positive connection.

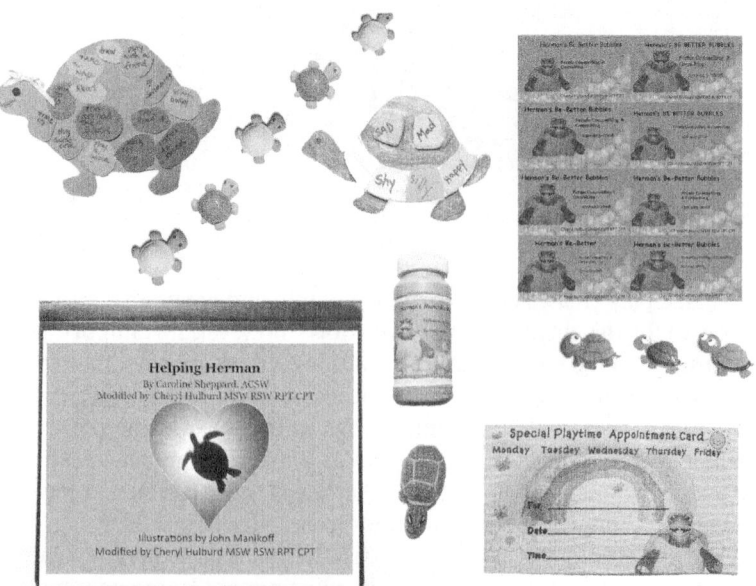

Figure 7.2 Turtles – here, there, and everywhere

Figure 7.3 Dan Siegel's diagram of the River of Well-Being (left) Herman's River of Well-Being (right)

I created Special Playtime Appointment cards with Herman's image on them and they are distributed at the end of the session. Sometimes Betsy and Lucy, my therapy dogs who help in the playroom, are also on the card. This card can provide a reminder of Herman when the child is at home. Caregivers can ask the child, "What would Herman say?"

Learning about the brain helps children understand their behavior. This may eliminate possible shame, confusion, and guilt from anger outbursts or sabotaging behaviors. Chapter 2 discussed Siegel and Bryson's (2011) description of mind integration and mindsight. The photo from his book *The Whole Brain Child* illustrated balance as being centered in a river. I refined this lesson by using Herman in their illustration. I explain to the child that Herman is centered and balanced and when the child is also centered and balanced, they too can "go with the flow."

PAPT and Engagement

During engagement, PAPT offers a foolproof method to convince children to follow a therapist into their office. As a social work student in training I witnessed a child who was reacting out of fear and displayed acting out behaviors in the hallway while being dragged into a therapy room. At the time I thought there must be another way. I discovered the better way while utilizing PAPT and labeled it the "Peek a Boo Engagement Technique."

The following is an example of how I used Herman with a young boy named Rikki. He was brought to my office because of shyness and struggles with social connections at school.

During the first session I observed that Rikki retreated behind his mother when I entered the waiting room. I engaged his mother in a discussion about play therapy and talked about my wonderful room full of toys. I tried to entice Rikki with a description of my playroom with no success. I explained that it was perfectly okay for him not to come in today and when he was feeling more adventurous, he was welcome to come back. I suggested that before they left, they meet my cotherapist puppet and I went into my office to retrieve Herman. I returned with my cotherapist puppet. I tried to introduce Herman to Rikki, but Herman refused to come out of his shell to meet him. He said he was too scared. I told Herman that it was common to be scared in new situations when meeting new people and tried to entice him out with ice cream. After more chatting with Herman about coming out of his shell, he finally did a quick pop out. Rikki was peeking over his mother's shoulder, and laughed when he saw Herman pop out. Hence, the development of "Peek a Boo." He played with Herman for a while in the waiting room until Herman finally announced that he was leaving to go into the playroom with his toys. Herman invited Rikki to come play with him and we slowly began to walk out of the waiting room into the playroom. During the transition from the waiting room to the play therapy room Rikki laughed and the three of us began our first session.

Future counseling appointments at "Herman's House" became an anticipated event rather than a fearful activity. Rikki's interactions with Herman, and other therapeutic activities during counseling, were the beginning of his social interactions and he was able to make many friends in his class. His mother reports that he is a bright, engaged, and energetic child that loves to learn and continues his growth and healthy development.

I created an adaptation to this technique that I use with Herman. Following the game of "Peek a Boo" that was mentioned earlier, if a child is still reluctant to engage once they are in the playroom, I introduce the, "Want some Ice Cream?" game. Herman goes back into his shell and is *too shy* to peek out again. I entice Herman to emerge with coaxing and offer him ice cream if he will return. Herman loves ice cream. He appears briefly and then ducks back down after I suggest a flavor of ice cream that he is not keen for. I offer a different flavor, and he comes out a little further, but decides to submerge again, not totally

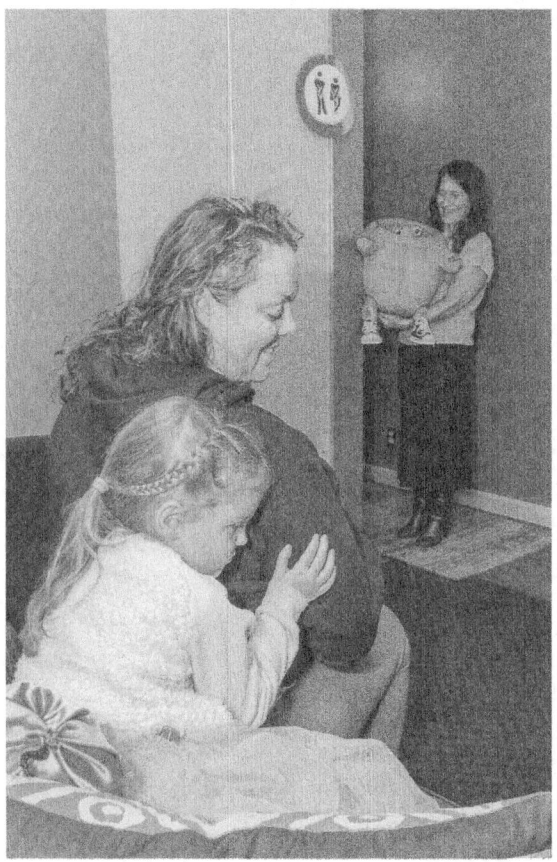

Figure 7.4 "Peek a Boo" game

buying into the second flavor. Then I recommend and sell another flavor. Herman gets excited and pops up enthusiastically.

In the event an extremely withdrawn child resists engagement in the playroom, I facilitate the projective process with Herman. Herman symbolizes the struggle that the child is experiencing. I have Herman say in a frightened voice, "I don't want to talk. I am too scared." I validate Herman's feelings and explain that in my playroom everything is okay and it is fine if he chooses not to talk. I tell Herman he is welcome to decide if and when he says anything. I comfort Herman by sharing that I am enjoying his company whether he speaks or not. This is an effective procedure to begin with selective mute children as well. After a while, Herman begins to whisper to me. This empowers the child, and

Figure 7.5 "The Girls" (Betsy and Lucy) working

eventually the child begins to whisper. I might even ask the child if they can help me understand how Herman is feeling.

If further engagement is required, I might facilitate further projection by having Herman ask, "What do I say or do now?" And I respond that he is free to choose to do anything he would like in almost any way he would like in this playroom.

Bow (1993) described another means of overcoming child resistance that he calls the "Hidden Puppet Technique." In this technique, the therapist hides a puppet in a sack or basket and encourages the child to help coax the resistant puppet out (Kaduson & Schaefer, 1997).

Engagement is an opportune time to introduce my other helpers in the office, Betsy and Lucy. These Bouvier des Flanders canines complement famously with the puppets. Herman now has others to check in with. It is entertaining and charming to observe the children interact with both Herman and Betsy and Lucy. "The girls" join the fun with Herman and sit in as the audience for the puppet shows when needed.

PAPT and Assessment

According to Irwin (1985); "In clinical work with children, the use of puppets has been invaluable both diagnostically and therapeutically [as an intervention] because of the richness of the symbolic material elicited in the spontaneous play" (p. 23). Puppet play is a great diagnostic tool. Puppets can enhance the assessment process by revealing significant information. The child's ego system, their defenses, intelligence, creativity, attention span, relational skills, problem-solving skills, cognitive abilities, interpersonal skills, and other facets of their development are exposed during puppet play.

A diagnostic assessment using puppets was developed by Irwin and Shapiro (1975). Sweeney and Homeyer (1999) further described this highly structured process, explaining that puppets are used in diagnosis because of their appeal and projective value. In this method, the therapist prompts the child to choose a puppet(s) and make up a story.

Following the puppet show, the therapist conducts an interview with the child and puppet characters. "By looking at the length and complexity of story, images, vocabulary, sentence structure, and story content, the therapist is able to make a diagnosis" (Sweeney, 2009, pp. 268–69). The storyline, themes, and content of the puppet show can produce abundant clues about the child from their strengths and weaknesses to their wishes and fears. "Examination of the story material, especially in the ways in which the child attempts to manage the feelings that emerge, give clues about the child's use of defenses, and aid in the developing an assessment picture" (Irwin, 1985, p. 395). Assessment is an ongoing process throughout treatment. Several PAPT techniques can be used for assessment and diagnostics. The geno-puppet-o-gram mentioned in Chapter 6 (see Figure 6.1, page 45) is a great way to begin.

Diagnostics that work for the individual child can also be implemented for family assessment. To help work with the family system, Irwin (1985) created a technique using puppets called "The Family Puppet Interview."

Here is a basket of puppets. Take a few minutes to look through them and choose a few that interest you. The instructions are to have the family tell a story with a beginning, middle and end. Try to decide how the story might begin. It is important that this story be a made-up story, not one that you have seen or read. There are two rules, you must make-up the story together and you must act it out rather than narrate. Take some time to make up the story and rehearse it and let me know when you are ready and I will be the audience as you tell me your story.

(Irwin, 1985, p. 24)

Numerous puppets are beneficial for this approach.

For the PAPT therapist, this technique allows a window into the decision making within the family, family patterns, and a chance to study symbolic communication between and amongst family members.

While working with a child during the family puppet interview, it is vital to stay in the puppet metaphor. Dialogue with the puppets in the story, not the family members. By staying in the metaphor, the clinician encourages the family to stay with their right hemisphere activity, delaying the more analytical and evaluative cognitions. It's not always necessary to rush to cerebral activity when you have an opportunity to deepen symbol or metaphor work first (Gil, APT convention 2010).

Gil offered several suggestions for dialogue in order to discuss the puppet play, come to a consensus, or find out something about one of the characters in the story. For example,

> "What's it like for the butterfly to watch all the action below? What does the butterfly notice about how the animals get along? How did it feel along the way?" Other examples would be: "Besides being mean, loud and fast, what other things do the spider and wolf have in common? When they aren't competing, what other things can they do together?" If an alien is involved, questions could be: "What's the alien's planet like? What's it like for the alien to visit planet earth? What would she like to say or do if she could reach the butterfly? How could the alien achieve...? Can the alien do ... rather than ....?" The child will project onto the puppet.
>
> (Gil, 2010)

The family puppet show (Irwin, 1985) is instrumental in family assessment. This interactive procedure has been beneficial in assessing the family without a history-taking interview. It illustrates the family's decision-making process and is useful in observing family patterns during conflicts or communications. The conflicts portrayed through the story are a wealth of information. "In the make-believe aspect of play families can often be helped to play, fantasize and look at family functioning in a non-threatening way" (Irwin, 1985, p. 33). This helps the therapist's direction and treatment. These authors outlined three steps to the interview.

1. To start the family puppet interview, the therapist might say, "The purpose of our meeting is to get to know you as a family. One way to become better acquainted is to ask you to do something together." Then ask the family to work together to make up an original story using a basket of puppets.
2. When the story is completed or stopped, the therapist can intervene by talking directly to the puppets or suggesting that certain puppets talk to each other about problem areas in the story. The therapist can pursue conflicts between puppets and explore significant themes as they appeared in the story, effecting closure if needed.

3. During post-play discussion, the therapist asks how the story might remind them of their own lives (Irwin, 1985, p. 25).

Another fun assessment activity is the PAPT Bird-day Party. I use Vern, my Bird-day puppet (the "Flight-ciatrist") for this activity. The Bird Birthday Party is an adaptation of Happy Birthday presented in Liana Lowenstein's (2002, p 99) book, *More Creative Interventions for Troubled Children and Youth*. Materials used for this activity are birthday paraphernalia, such as birthday decorations, party hats, horns, games, treats, and perhaps even a birthday cake. Decorate the room for a party and spread out a large selection of puppets. The puppet representing the child will sit at the head of the table. Place a chair at each table setting around the table. Have the child seat his "guests" in the preferred locations next to him at the table. Identify the individual puppets as guests representing different people in their life that they would like at the party. Who is next to them? Who is not there? The child gives each puppet a voice commenting on the party or about the birthday child puppet (which is a representation of the child).

Projection is a popular assessment technique that works well with PAPT. Children project feelings into/onto any object or story of focus. Oaklander (1978) specified that projection unravels fantasies, anxieties, fears, avoidances, frustrations, attitudes, patterns, manipulations,

Figure 7.6 Vern's Assessment Bird-day Party

impulses, resistances, resentments, guilt, wishes, wants, needs, and feelings. Often times it is sufficient to expose these, which facilitates emotional growth.

When a child explains the problems that they are experiencing, the therapist must experience and hold these emotions for the child, whether it be pain, anger, sadness, or conflict (Oaklander, 1978).

In my practice, one of my favorite projection interventions is Oaklander's Rosebush Fantasy. I adapted this intervention to be used with my rose puppet, whose name is Rose. I select Rose, for this fantasy and she says, "Hi. I was picked just to be with you." Oaklander (1978) recommended questions like:

> Can you tell me what kind of rosebush you are? Are you small? Are you large? Are you fat? Are you tall? Do you have flowers? If so, what kind (they don't have to be roses)? What color are your flowers? Do you have many or just a few? Are you in full bloom or do you only have buds? Do you have leaves? What kind? What are your stems and branches like? What are you roots like...or maybe you don't have any? If you do, are they long and straight? Are they twisted? Are they deep? Do you have thorns? Where are you? In a yard? Park? In the desert? In the city? In the country? In the middle of the ocean? Are you in a pot or growing in the ground or through cement? Or even inside somewhere? What is around you? Are there other flowers or are you alone? Are there trees? Animals? People? Birds? Do you look like a rosebush or something else? Is there anything around you like a fence? If so, what is it like? Or are you just in an open place? What's it like to be a rosebush? How do you survive? Does someone take care of you? What is the weather for you like right now?
>
> (p. 33)

I then ask the child if the answers fit into her own life. This technique is both diagnostic and used for assessment or as an intervention to approach significant issues in the child's life. A therapist will most likely find that a child's life is an amazing replication of this exercise. The children find it easier and more fun to engage with a rose puppet than to simply answer questions from a therapist. Supplemental assessments can be extrapolated from the puppet play. The puppet characters can be drawn for additional assessment techniques.

PAPT and Interventions

Intervention is the next stage in the therapeutic process. PAPT can aid in numerous ways in this stage. Many techniques mentioned in prior chapters can be used as intervention techniques. This section presents unique interventions.

These additional methods can further your PAPT repertoire and include mending a broken heart, the TV interview, and bibliotherapy. Adaptations and transformations of these and other methods will evolve as you discover how your present practice ideas merge with PAPT. Herman teaching feelings is paramount in healing as an intervention. Learning to identify and express feelings is fundamental for PAPT and this intervention is the building block of therapy.

The effectiveness of imagery as a PAPT mindfulness exercise was illustrated by a child who came to my practice who was being bullied at school. Animal puppets were presented in the playroom. I asked the child if he could choose any of these animals while he was being bullied, which one would he choose? The child chose the dragon. He said the dragon would be with him in front of the bullies and breathe fire as a way of protecting him.

The therapist invites the child to fantasize about the situation and problem solving can be implemented by the child. Their imagery creates what is needed for them.

Examples of things to ask a child:

- "Pick a puppet that you would like to be today."
- "Show me what happened and how your puppet could help."
- "How can this animal help you with your problem?"

In this particular PAPT intervention, SIFT (sensations, images, feelings, and thoughts) is very useful to help the child process the

Figure 7.7 PAPT imagery of inner strength

experience of being bullied and what it felt like to be powerful versus powerless.

When children learn to be specific with feelings and emotions, they can move from vague emotional descriptors like fine and bad to more precise ones like anxious, jealous, and excited. Children don't express the complexity of a specific emotion because they haven't learned to think of their feelings in a sophisticated enough way to recognize the variety and richness within them.

"They [children] don't use full spectrum emotions in their responses and paint their emotional pictures in black and white. We want our kids to recognize that there is a colorful rainbow of rich emotions within them and pay attention to these different possibilities. When they have a full emotional palette, they are able to experience the vivid Technicolor that a deep and vibrant life allows" (Seigel and Bryson, 2011, p. 106).

Research shows that merely assigning a name or label to what we feel literally calms down the activity of the emotional circuitry in the right hemisphere of the brain (Siegel & Bryson, 2011). Some children are not familiar with what feelings are. This may seem odd because all children can feel their emotions intensely, but they have a limited ability to understand and communicate these feelings. They also tend to see things as black and white. I find it helpful to introduce a variety of feelings and their distinctions and degrees. Children need to be able to identify what their feelings are and understand that everyone has feelings. In the playroom we discuss how it is healthy to share, express, and talk about our feelings. For children who do not express these feelings, the subsequent emotions can lead to unhealthy behaviors, thoughts, or somatic symptoms. Children also need to learn they can make choices about ways of expressing their feelings.

Herman the Turtle puppet teaches feelings by explaining the benefits of our emotions, as well as ways to regulate them. He explains that way down deep, feelings exist in us for different reasons and that feelings accompany our experiences. Sometimes he has more than one feeling at a time. Sometimes he gets angry. I ask the child, "Do you think it's ok to be angry like Herman? What makes you angry? How do you show it when you are angry? How does it feel in your body? Where do you feel it? Herman wants to know what you do when you feel it?"

Herman discusses the relationship of the body to feelings and explains that all the feelings are experienced through body sensations (where and how you feel the feeling in your body). We tune in further to Herman's body so the child becomes aware of where emotions are felt in his own body and what they are doing with their body at the moment they express a feeling. Tuning into the body can tell a child and warn a child what they are feeling. Similarly, the child can begin to recognize the body sensations they are experiencing as a smoke detector to understand they may be headed out of the window of tolerance.

Herman explains that whether or not we talk about these feelings, our body still stores the feelings. It is only when we acknowledge our feelings and experience them (process them) that we can release them. This way we can use our mind, heart, and body for other things in our lives. If we do not release them, but rather ignore, avoid, or hide our feelings, a part of us continually holds onto these feelings, leaving us with only part of ourselves for living and experiencing ongoing life experiences. Herman explains that it is important to listen to our bodies to help experience our feelings and listen to our feelings to help experience our bodily sensations. Body, posture, facial expressions, and gestures are all included in this discussion.

Herman has "feelings buttons" in his shell that children reach in for and pull out. Many get reprimanded by Herman for tickling him when they reach in. Herman does not like to be tickled. Again, the game of SIFT supplements this lesson of learning feelings and how feelings or emotions are manifested and held in our body. When children practice mindsight, they can take control of feelings and learn to diminish the power they have over them.

An intervention technique Herman uses for grieving is an adaption of Lowenstein's (2008) technique called "Your Heart." This activity was created for children grieving over a loved one's death. In my practice, I have adapted this technique with Herman. Herman has a broken heart inside that has been glued together. The child pulls out the heart from Herman's shell and we explore what has happened to the heart.

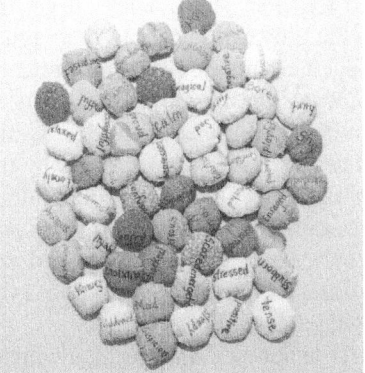

Figure 7.8 Herman sharing his feelings using feelings buttons

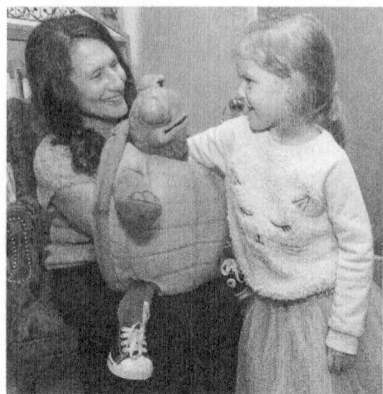

Figure 7.9 Herman helping to mend a broken heart

We discuss how the heart is different. Herman's broken heart represents many types of loss. Lowenstein describes this as being "not exactly the same as it was before the death... The marks are like scars on one's heart ... it's stronger now, and it will never be quite the same after a death... in time the scars will actually help a child think of all the good memories they had with the special person who died" (2008, p. 97).

PAPT can be utilized in group settings as well. Mutual Storytelling through Puppet Play in Group Play Therapy (MSTPP) was developed by Richard Gardner (as cited in Kaduson & Schaefer, 1997). This form of PAPT is an intervention that uses children's stories about the challenges that led them to seek treatment. Each child in the group chooses one animal puppet that shows how they feel and is most able to tell their story. They all get together with their animals and plan what they will say about their abuse. They pretend they are in the forest together and are sitting around a campfire talking. Each child tells their story using this puppet and gets support from the other puppets. The puppets can encourage details and tell how they protect themselves. The children discover that they may share similar stories and identify with the feelings being acted out. As a result of sharing, they may feel reassured that their feelings are accepted and experience increased self-confidence. The therapist and cotherapist puppet introduce coping strategies in order to assist with their unresolved conflicts (Kaduson & Schaefer, 1997).

Elementary schools may benefit from this technique, concentrating on common school issues such as bullying, aggression, isolation, and withdrawal. Many other issues in various milieus can be addressed with this group technique. A therapist should be aware this technique may be contraindicated for severely abused children who might experience revictimization and retraumatization through the reenactment of the abuse through puppet play.

PAPT and Termination

Termination, the last component of the therapeutic process, is the development of a summary of what has been accomplished in treatment as well as honoring the farewell component. Puppets may be used in several ways to recap therapy during termination.

I sewed smaller turtle puppets that I introduce as Herman's cousin and these are given to each child. We practice labeling the feelings buttons for their own turtle puppet and play the same feelings game we played with Herman. After the therapy session, the children take

Figure 7.10 Herman's cousin sharing feelings

home this support puppet to continue to play their feelings games. The pattern for these puppets is included in Appendix B.

To create the written feelings, I use sheets of foam and cut them into small circles the size of quarters. The children help me write feelings on the circles and then we place these foam circles inside the puppet's shell. I give blank foam circles to the families to assure therapeutic continuity. Caregivers can add new and different feelings to these puppets as needed.

Rise Van Fleet has developed a popular play therapy technique that is useful in the intervention and termination stages. She calls it "The TV Interview." Van Fleet presented this technique at the Center for Play Therapy Conference at the University of Texas (Texas, 2004). Two microphones, a video camera and a telephone (I use Herman's "shell phone") are needed for this technique. A room with a table is set up as if we were on a radio talk show. Herman or another puppet is the host. The child is the "expert of the show." Callers (the therapist) from a pretend audience call in. The callers use different silly voices each time the phone rings. The caller asks questions about any struggles they may have that are pertinent to the child's recovery. For instance, "What should I do when I am bullied at school?" or "What should I do when my mom and dad are fighting and hurting each other?" The child

Figure 7.11 TV Interview termination technique – broadcasting advice by the experts

responds with his newfound knowledge regarding the caller's dilemma. The video is used to tape the show so it can be watched by the therapist and the child when the show is over.

Most children love this technique, though there are exceptions. I created a variation to this technique with a timid child, Susan, who refused to talk. Susan went under the table and held her chosen puppet, the wise old owl, to sit on the table. She talked through the wise old owl puppet. She ended up answering a different question on each topic every time Herman's "shell phone" rang. Susan gained confidence as she answered questions through the Wise Old Owl. Betsy and Lucy also supported Susan during the show.

Although animal puppets are preferred in my playroom, object puppets can be used as well. Flowers, trees, or shells are great adaptions. Perhaps they are more popular due to the fact that they are three times removed through therapeutic distance.

8 Even More PAPT Techniques and Interventions

I would like to elaborate on several techniques mentioned earlier that are unique to PAPT. These techniques include bibliotherapy, puppet meditation, deep breathing exercises, imagery in the ocean, and storytelling.

PAPT and Bibliotherapy

When a play therapist uses books to read stories to children, the process is known as bibliotherapy. Bibliotherapy is defined as "literature to bring about a therapeutic interaction between a participant and a facilitator" (Hynes & Hynes-Berry, 1994). Bibliotherapy is effective because readers identify with the characters and children can work through a problem along with the character, ultimately achieving insight about their own situations (Pehrsson, 2006).

Indirectly and cautiously, literature offers advice and recommendations for decision making and helps children communicate more openly. The books provide a distance, a kind of safety net for emotional intensity, a buffer that children often need (Pehrsson, 2006).

PAPT is a perfect medium to use with bibliotherapy. Children can use puppets to identify with the characters in the book. Books offer safe therapeutic distancing as well as put words to issues that children cannot. Advantages and outcomes of bibliotherapy, such as problem solving, creativity, expression, and mastery, align well with the benefits of PAPT. Adaptations can be made from original storyline characters to fit any puppet characters in your playroom. Instead of cats stretching, you can use the storyline for dogs. Dogs stretch too. An owl can meditate to replace a cow, and so on.

Examples of books that work well with PAPT:

Cool Cats, Calm Kids: Relaxation and Stress Management for Young People by Williams and O'Quinn Burke (2007). Children love to perform these exercises with their cat or kitten puppets. In this book cats share various strategies to calm and relax. And children can utilize these exercise strategies along with their cat puppets. Exercises include stretching, taking a cat nap, and meowing together.

A Mother for Choco by Kasza (1992) is a story about adoption, which I tell using baby bird puppets.

Brave Bart, by Caroline Sheppard (1998), is a story about trauma and how it affects Bart. I adapted *Brave Bart* for Herman with permission from W. Steele from the National Institute for Trauma and Loss for Children. The cat was substituted with Herman the Turtle and my book *Helping Herman* is now in several different languages. Turtle puppets are playing out trauma in numerous countries around the world.

Dear Bear, a book by Joanna J. Harrison (1994), is a warm-hearted story about becoming friends with nightmare characters. A mother helps her daughter befriend the scary bear in the closet by eventually having a tea party with him after letters are exchanged with the little girl in the story. Several bear puppets are used in the playroom.

The Little Engine That Could by Piper (1930) relates a story about the success of perseverance. The train puppets are popular with small children.

Kerry Lee MacLean's *Moody Cow Meditates* (2009) and *Peaceful Piggy Meditation* (2004) teach children how to meditate. A pig and cow meditate with children in the playroom.

Figure 8.1 Little Engine finger puppets

Don't Feed the Monster on Tuesdays!: The Children's Self-Esteem Book by Adolph Moser (1991), is a favorite book on self-esteem and assists with teaching affirmations.

Eggbert, the Slightly Cracked Egg by Tom Ross (2002) is a story about an egg with a slight injury that is taunted and cast out of the refrigerator and into the world. Eggbert's journey helps him realize that there are cracks everywhere and reminds us that our cracks are perfectly natural. This book has been used with trauma survivors who perceive themselves as different because of their hidden wounds.

Figure 8.2 Don't Feed the Monster. (The Green Monster puppet and others can be purchased at www.ferniecounselling.ca)

As mentioned earlier, when the concept of strengths perspective was introduced, the book *The Enchanted Tree* by Weedn and Weedn (1995) became a favorite. Yes, I have an enchanted tree puppet in my playroom. This resource focuses on positive self-esteem, correcting cognitive distortions, and is often used in my office with all the puppets from the story: the enchanted tree puppet, the giraffe puppet, the owl puppet, and of course the turtle.

Therapeutic Stories that Teach and Heal by Nancy Davis (1966) is a favorite resource for children. It is a thorough and complete work that addresses most issues that occur in the playroom.

The above-mentioned books are by no means an inclusive list. Lots of wonderful books have been published that work well with PAPT. Therapists can go through their own books or create a story book that is unique to their own clientele. I have acquired and created many puppets for my own practice, however, PAPT can be used with fewer puppets. If you already have puppets in the playroom, you most likely have many of the characters you need.

Though numerous stories feature turtles in my practice, most stories for children feature other characters and animals in their storyline. Be creative and use your imagination when it comes to using PAPT in your own practice.

PAPT and Meditation

Research in neuroscience has determined that meditation practitioners shift brain activity to different areas of the brain (Davidson et al., 2003). Researchers discovered that brain waves in the frontal cortex switched sides of the brain. Neuroscientists theorize that this shift decreases the negative effects of stress, mild depression, and anxiety. They also found less activity in the amygdala, where the brain processes the debilitating emotion of fear. The benefits of meditation can effectively increase mental health by helping children alleviate stress and increase feelings of self-esteem (Fisher, 2006). A combination of meditation, puppetry, and bibliotherapy increases therapeutic value.

PAPT and Imagery

Deep breathing exercises using bubbles were mentioned earlier. Exercises combining deep breathing with imagery can double the efficacy when a puppet and/or puppet theme are paired with guided imagery.

Fantasy trips are another effective medium for PAPT and guided imagery. One fantasy trip that I commonly use is adapted from *101*

More Favorite Play Therapy Techniques (Kaduson & Schaefer, 1997). I renamed the technique "The Great Turtle Adventure." Following is my script.

"I invite you to take an imaginative healing trip with Herman. Close your eyes and take big, deep breaths. In your imagination, let yourself become a sea turtle, just like Herman. We are at the ocean and Herman wants you to come for a swim with him and his friends.

"As you are swimming, feel yourself gliding effortlessly though the water. Smell the salty air. Picture yourself being held up by the water, floating along. Now, dive deep and see what other creatures are swimming in the deep ocean. Notice the gentle pull of the current as you drift towards the soothing calm. Blow rhythmic bubbles as you descend to the bottom. Now, attach your flipper to Herman's shell and go for a ride back up to the warm blue sparkling water. Feel the sunlight penetrating the water and you. As you swim up to the surface, look up to the blue sky and cottony clouds. What do they look like? Can you see your favorite animal in the clouds? Another one? Notice the warmth on your shell from the sun. Can you hear the seagulls off in the distance? Listen to them sing. They are approaching you. One black seagull swoops down and you give him all of your angries. He takes them away up into the sky. You watch him majestically fly into the big white fluffy clouds forever. He is gone – along with your angries. You are peaceful now with them gone. You move towards the light. You are safe. You feel lighter. You drift along the shoreline with Herman and notice an oyster. You pry it open with your powerful flipper and there is a small white glimmering pearl inside. You find this special gift. It is magic! This magic pearl makes you feel special and loved and grants wishes of happy feelings. As long as you hold this pearl in your thoughts, your wish of happy feelings will make you smile. This is your happy place. This swim with Herman will always be with you and remind you of good times to come. You are filled with joy. The sun is shining brightly. As you continue your journey you can feel the magic and share your smiles with your other turtle friends. Now you feel relaxed and happy from your day's adventure at the sea with Herman. Take a deep breath and come back to visit Herman in the playroom. Open your eyes and stretch and reach for the sky."

Have the child use a puppet show to tell you about the experience. This imagery exercise of Herman's turtle trip can also be transposed into the SIFT game. The therapist can say, "Stop. Let's listen to the ocean's waves and float. What are you seeing, smelling, hearing, and feeling, and experiencing right now?"

PAPT and Storytelling

Healing and change can be about learning new perspectives and reviewing what was learned. Puppet storytelling is a powerful tool for conveying a therapist's intention or message and scientific research confirms this. Storytelling can convert implicit memories into explicit memories and integrate the brain.

Storytelling has an amazing effect on the brain. According to Uri Hanson from Princeton (as cited in Oberoi, 2014), we link metaphors and literal happenings automatically. Everything in our brains is searching for the cause and effect relationship to something that we have previously experienced. His research showed that when listening to another person speak and tell a story the same areas of both speakers' and listeners' brains light up in an MRI exam. I wonder if Herman's brain does also.

According to this article, "the results showed that not only did all the listeners show similar brain activity during the story, the speaker and listener had very similar brain activity despite the fact that one person was producing language and the others were comprehending" (Oberoi, 2014). The front cortex, the area of the brain responsible for experiencing emotions, is activated with stories we are able to relate to. The specific imageries influence perception and infer outcome.

The story Oberoi told was about his experiment in storytelling. He merged storytelling with sales. He purchased inexpensive items on eBay and resold them with a story. Merely by telling an emotional story about the item the shoppers were engaged and motivated to buy his items for a 625% markup (Widrich, 2012). From this experiment, imagine what accomplishments a puppet could do in your playroom with a good story.

The storytelling process makes addressing a child's feelings less scary. The storyteller can offer some control over what a child deals with so the child can interact with it at their own pace. Puppets can be used to reenact the experiences into a story in a way that provides opportunity to visit the characters' sensations, images, feelings, and thoughts (SIFT) in the story. This helps the child relate to his own SIFT. Storytelling with puppets creates new experiences for a child's brain to integrate. A visit to the hospital may now feel more familiar to them. They know what to expect, which decreases the anxiety of the unknown. Having the child choose the puppet character for the therapist's story can be even more effective.

There are other adaptations for PAPT that can complement and enhance your play therapy practice. One example, *Powerful Puppetry* by Saenz (2002), includes different games, activities, and plays to use with puppets. The power of puppets is evolving in playrooms across the globe. Children exhibit deep and passionate communication with puppets. Witnessing therapeutic puppetry in the playroom is witnessing magic. Techniques and interventions can easily be adapted to address the needs of each child with your puppets.

9 PAPT and Specific Issues in Play Therapy

Several PAPT interventions are effective in addressing specific issues that arise in the playroom. These include medical puppet play, abuse disclosure, and custody evaluation.

PAPT and Medical Puppet Play

Medical PAPT is a method that can assist numerous children who find themselves being treated by medical professionals. Puppets help solidify the information of forthcoming procedures in a fun, effective way by providing safe therapeutic distance. An adaptation intervention from *Child Parent Relationship Therapy (CPRT) Treatment Manual* (Bratton et al., 2006) can be transformed into PAPT. The CPRT treatment manual suggests beginning structuring doll play that matches the upcoming stressful event.

Structured doll play can provide a short and focused experience for children to prepare themselves for a medical procedure or other anxiety-provoking experience. Creative storytelling using puppets rather than dolls is a compelling way for parents to help children who are feeling anxious or insecure. Prior to a medical intervention, a puppet can be used to demonstrate the purpose of a procedure and to illustrate exactly what is involved. The puppet goes through the upcoming experience, titrating the scheduled procedure. Since the child is holding a puppet, the intervention can be replayed using only the child's hand. This can be easier on the child than involving their whole body because the puppet can share the pain or explain how the pain may be affecting them. This PAPT technique can also be used for any stressful change that is expected, such as a parent's divorce, explaining a funeral or graveside service, visiting a patient in the hospital, a change in location and school, or a new addition to the family.

Introduce the characters, tell the story, and have a beginning, a middle, and an end to the message. It is helpful to keep the questions and dialogue in metaphor.

Figure 9.1 Is there a doctor in the house?

Researchers have suggested that therapeutic play for hospitalized children can be a useful approach to reducing psychological distress related to the experience of illness and hospitalization. Medical puppet play is perfect for this therapeutic play (Loftin, 2018).

PAPT and Abuse Disclosure

It is paramount that the child knows you must report any acts of harm, so they do not feel betrayed. When a child does not take the time to build a relationship with the therapist but begins traumatic play immediately, this indicates that the abuse is still current. Immediately entering into traumatic play without a relationship with the therapist is a way of crying out for help. Norton and Norton (1997) prefaced this by asserting that immediate traumatic play occurs when the pain from the trauma is greater than the need for the relationship. Reactions and responses may dictate the future and have serious setbacks. Careful, proficient, and well-trained actions at this time are critical.

Child victims of abuse generally have been groomed well and are fearful to come forward. They have been coached not to tell anyone about the abuse and the coaching can range from invoking sympathy (I will lose my job and my family will be hungry) to threatening harm (I will kill your family). The nature of a child is that they cannot, not tell. The disclosure happens in a way that makes sense to the child, such as, "I don't want to go to Grandpa's anymore," but does not always trigger alarm for the caregiver. Sometimes they do not have the vocabulary or understanding to explain what is happening to them. Acting out the scenarios using puppets to tell their story is less anxiety producing.

It is a very courageous effort to disclose. It must be easier to tell a turtle than a person. Puppets are the best way to get a disclosure. It is essential that the stage of change is recognized for the disclosure to occur. Victims usually appear in our office at the contemplation stage.

The stages of change are as follows:

1. Pre-contemplation (Not yet acknowledging that there is a problem – behavior that needs to be changed);
2. Contemplation (Acknowledging that there is a problem but not yet ready or sure of wanting to make a change);
3. Preparation/Determination (Getting ready to change);
4. Action/Willpower (Changing behavior);
5. Maintenance (Maintaining the behavior change); and
6. Relapse (Returning to older behaviors and abandoning the new changes) (AddictionInfo, n.d.).

Storing a secret may be the first step to help move a disclosure along. Questions asked to identify the perpetrator can hinder therapy. Forensic questioning in the inappropriate stages of therapy is counterproductive to the therapeutic outcomes of the child. Direct questioning can have the effect of pulling the child out of his or her protective fantasy play and forcing them into the reality of their experiences. This violates the protection provided by the therapist in their relationship with the child. When this happens, the therapeutic process can be permanently damaged. A possible dialogue with PAPT may be something like the following.

A nurse puppet could say: "Have you ever had a splinter? Have you ever had a splinter you couldn't see? They hurt, don't they? Do you know how to stop them from hurting? They stop hurting when you take it out. Do you know what a yucky secret is? It is a secret that hurts, and it feels yucky. Can you imagine how to stop a yucky secret from hurting? Yes, it needs to come out. You can get it out by telling a friend or giving it to friend like this." I introduce this turtle who has a zippered mouth. I show them that this puppet can zip the secret. "You can give it to this turtle by writing on this paper or drawing a picture and then zipping it in this friend's mouth."

The nurse shares that "Sometimes grownups say that you will get in trouble if you tell one of their secrets ... but they are tricks. You won't really get into trouble. Did anyone ever try and trick you like that?" Watch for body language. "Let's make a list of anything that is yucky or poopy in your life." Sometimes kids use my friends/puppets to help talk to me if they are scared. If there is reluctance to continue, perhaps you can offer that maybe there is a braver friend/puppet. "Would you like to pick a friend? Is there any secret that is yucky or poopy and hard for you to tell? Maybe we need someone braver." Ask the child if they would like to pick another puppet. Some kids have secrets about being touched. Attention to timing is critical if you ever have to ask a child about touching. "Is it a touching secret?" Talk to the puppet, not the child. Various animals can be used. Use your imagination. A snail, a kangaroo, a turtle, a dog, a cat, an elephant or even a Siberian tiger puppet can elicit information. The idea is to have their friend puppet tell my friend puppet about their experience.

PAPT and Custody Evaluation

Custody Evaluation when paired with PAPT demonstrates profound truths necessary for accurate child's view reports.

Technique and Dialogue

A client named Henry once came to "Herman's House" when his parents were in a high-conflict divorce. As his mother was addicted to and still using drugs, she was allowed supervised visits only. Henry lived with his father. The visits were not going well because the mother would not cooperate with the supervisors, and Henry was becoming more distraught. He was emotionally unregulated and becoming aggressive. He did not want to continue with the supervised visits at his mother's house. Prior to leaving my office, he requested that I tell the judge that he did not want to continue with visits to see his mother.

I suggested that he return the following week and told him that *he* could be the one to tell the judge. After he left, I got busy sewing. At the next visit, I introduced Henry to Judge Herman.

Henry loved it. I suggested that we make a movie for fun. The video camera recorded the entire session. He sat down and told the judge everything that had transpired and how he felt. I explained to Henry that we now needed a jury. I explained the function of the jury. I then surrounded the table with several chairs and asked him to choose the puppets he wanted to fill the chairs with as the jurors. One was another turtle puppet, another a large ugly witch puppet – an essential puppet for any playroom, because who doesn't have a witch in their life? As Henry sat the witch in her chair, he explained that the witch puppet was

Figure 9.2 Order in the court

his mother. I asked him to tell me about her, and he simply said that she is mean and ugly. He put a large cute dog puppet in the next chair as another juror. Henry patted the dog on its head and explained that this was his father. He hugged the dog. He filled the last chair with a sorcerer with a magic wand. I asked him what he was wishing for from this magician; he responded, "I wish for hot chocolate."

It is important to note that sessions to acquire child views for court reports cannot be coached by either parent, like many verbal interviews are. Raw, unrehearsed information is advised. In our mock courtroom, Henry spoke through each puppet. He was very insightful and believed that his mother truly wanted to spend time with him even though her nurturing behavior was lacking. Henry revealed that one visit with his mother had left him traumatized. His mother had locked him in his room and said she would pay him off with money and candy while she and her friends partied in the home. The supervisor could not enter the house as the front door was locked, and phoned the RCMP (police) who immediately came to the home. The mother encouraged Henry to jump out the back window with her to avoid the RCMP (they were on the first floor). Henry's stress level and trauma were apparent as he explained the scenario to the mock court.

Once the mock trial was over, Henry was given the gavel and he became the judge. He stated; "You need to spend time with both your mother and father. They both love you. Supervision is not working well at your mother's home so we should move the visits to a different place. We also need two supervisors." Henry was a remarkable four-year-old and an intelligent and practical judge.

This session was recorded on video. The judge was able to "see" what was happening clearly. In this particular scenario, witch and puppy puppets were chosen by the child to represent his mother (the witch) and his father (the puppy). It is crucial to have an assortment of puppets so that all children can find one that is relatable to them. Around 15 to 30 puppets is adequate for most children to express their stories, and these must represent a range of affects and an inclusion of real and fantasy puppets, as well as object puppets. The more puppets and props you have in your playroom the better children are able to represent their stories. There is definite truth to the saying: the more the merrier.

10 Puppet Making

This chapter will assist you in the process of puppet making by providing commonly utilized materials, informative resources, and a list of accessories for your puppets. Tips, techniques, and patterns are indexed. These ideas are designed to boost the readers' confidence in their ability to creatively implement puppet sessions with children in the playroom.

A discussion of therapeutic safety is appropriate when choosing and designing puppets. Puppets are successful because they create distance between the reenactment of difficult memories or experiences. Titration is required when addressing painful experiences. Children may begin processing such memories by projecting themselves onto toys or stuffed animals. At the next level of processing, puppets incorporate the memory or experience to a slightly more intrusive level, as the child is "wearing" the character. The closest medium is "dress up," where the child actually is the character.

There seems to be a similar safety progression strategy with puppets themselves. This titration is described by Ingram, and refers to people puppets as once removed, animal puppets as twice removed, and objects as three times removed. People puppets are used to reflect the different roles and genders of the characters involved. Animal puppets are used to display characters' moods, strengths, or personalities. Objects are used as symbolic archetypes – perhaps a flower, a sun, a tree, or a fast-talking car.

I have found that most children prefer animal puppets or inanimate object puppets over people puppets; however, it is helpful to have a variety of options to meet the needs of each unique child.

Most of the materials used in making puppets are commonly found in any household. Discarded items can be recycled with some imagination. Possible construction materials include socks, mittens, old blankets, fabrics, tongue depressors, paper bags, paper plates, construction paper, foam sheets, mops, brooms, googly eyes (peepers), and converted stuffed animals. I have even utilized a dish scrubby as an effective performer. The only limit in puppet making is the creativity of the maker.

A multitude of resources are available to learn about puppet making. Of course, the Internet is the most widely used; sites such as eBay and Amazon have numerous homemade puppet ideas and puppets for sale. OrientalTrading.com is a popular commercial site that distributes catalogues. Sewing stores offer a wide range of ideas, such as Fabricland in Canada or JOANN's Fabric Store in the US, a national chain found in most major shopping centers. JOANN's provides a complimentary puppet pattern for their customers, which is listed in Appendix B.

The art of puppet making began long before the use of puppets in the field of social work. Years ago, I created a teddy bear from my beloved mother's mink coat. I developed a business from the idea called Beirlooms – Huggable Heirlooms, where I transformed customers' treasured heirlooms into stuffed teddy bears. While I was pursuing my newfound interest in puppet making, Kermit, the Sesame Street puppet, entered the scene.

The earliest trace of Kermit first appeared in 1955 on WRC-TV's *Sam and Friends*. This prototype of Kermit was made by Jim Henson, the creator of Sesame Street. Kermit was created from a discarded spring coat that belonged to Henson's mother using two ping pong ball halves for eyes ("Kermit the Frog," 2019).

This story inspired me. I took another of my mother's old beloved heirloom mink coats and transformed it into a huggable Beirloom puppet, named Sylvia Ann as a legacy to her.

The same pattern I used for Sylvia Ann the Beirloom puppet inspired me to make a totally different character, Trixie. Again, anything a person can dream up can be a puppet.

Increased interest and involvement with puppets led me to pursue research in the art of puppetry. I learned about Jeff Dunham, a stand-up comedian, actor, and ventriloquist who has appeared on numerous TV shows, social media, and on his own TV series. Many of his videos are available on YouTube. Jeff Dunham's favorite puppet friend is Achmed the dead terrorist, which was transformed from a Halloween decoration skeleton into his famous ventriloquist puppet.

For those puppet creators who do not sew, alternative options are available. Glue is an effective means of construction. Velcro works too. Be aware that you will need an opening for hands or fingers in your puppet. The best puppets for children have smaller, user-friendly openings.

The Oriental Trading Company sells many reasonably priced puppet making kits.

"Sew with Joann" also offers several animal puppet patterns. Each pattern can easily be customized to meet your needs.

Figure 10.1 Mom's mink puppet pattern reused for other puppet characters

The basic turtle puppet pattern I use (Appendix B) can have more elaborate decorations. The basic pattern also allows for many other possible characters, including a rabbit, monster, lion, and house cat.

Creating tongue depressor puppets using photos of a child's family members glued to the edge can be an effective method. Even paper bags or paper plates can be converted into colorful puppets.

Now that you have your puppets, how to display them? Consider shoe bags, plastic chain, thread holders for finger puppets, shoe racks, homemade PVC racks, etc. Creative presentation and display techniques add a personalized touch to your playroom. Different activities require different presentations. For example, I implement the family puppet show on a large table and dump the puppets from a bag. This allows the therapist to watch the selection of puppets, family direction, and inclusion. Family direction may involve who controls the show, the storyline, and, in general, the family dynamics of creating the show. In a nondirective play therapy session, the child is welcome to hide behind the puppet stage and go through the puppets from a bin or shoe bag. A well-thought-out treatment plan aids in the display and presentation for each individual session and doesn't lose sight of the spontaneity and flexibility that play therapy requires.

Puppet presentation ideas can be as basic as a table or as elaborate as a commercial stage. Home-made puppet theaters to commercial doorway puppet theaters are all appreciated by the puppeteers.

Puppet props and costumes make puppet play more enticing and fun and can strengthen the bond between a child and the puppets. When children come into my office in the fall, they often show me their new school shoes, so Herman also shows his new school shoes. Other prop suggestions include skateboards, glasses, barbeque sets, sports, dance, fitness paraphilia, wands, crowns, and even EMDR tools (discussed further in Chapter 14). Build-A-Bear Workshop® sells excellent props and costumes for puppets.

Alternatively, you may give children basic puppet shapes to create their own puppets for their own therapeutic needs. One child may create a beautiful princess with a sparkly tierra, while another designs a scary one-eyed monster. The child projects his feelings, moods, and roles onto the creation process. The questions that you may ask following the construction of a puppet are helpful in all phases of therapy, from engagement and assessment to intervention and termination.

These children are encouraged to use these well-loved puppets at home.

11 The Art of Puppetry – Make Your Puppet Come Alive

Learning the basics of effective puppetry is essential to create an optimal experience with your new "coworker." The basics involve ventriloquism, movements, choosing the right puppets, using puppets correctly in the playroom, and methods for storing puppets.

The first rule in PAPT is to avoid having a "lifeless" puppet sitting in an office. The therapist, therefore, must learn two essential illusions; ventriloquism and the instillation of lifelike movements. It is crucial to explore and get in touch with your new cotherapist puppet. The puppet's nonverbal dimension – its appearance, moves, and sounds – must be convincing in order to connect with children.

The entrance and introduction of your cotherapist puppet is paramount. This crucial step establishes the life of the puppet and lets the child know that you are confident. Pull the puppet out of a suitcase, from behind a chair, or help it appear from inside its shell. In my office, Herman sits in a child's rocking chair next to my chair watching TV. His head is in his shell. When I first began using Herman, he had an antenna for his TV. One child continued to inquire about his antenna. I explained several times that he needed better reception when in his shell. I could not understand why the child was so perplexed until I realized that children today do not know what an antenna is!

I usually begin by asking Herman to please come out and meet my new friend. He generally doesn't want to come out of his shell because he is too shy. I ask the child to encourage Herman to come out to meet them. This immediate engagement between Herman and the child cements the bond between them.

I continue conversing with Herman. The conversation goes something like this:

ME: Herman, what were you watching on TV?
HERMAN: Franklin.
ME: Ooh, I love Franklin. Can you tell our new friend what we do for work?

Figure 11.1 Herman watches TV

HERMAN: Ok, but what are you doing now?
ME: Oh, this. This is called ventriloquism.
HERMAN: What's that?
ME: It's when I talk without moving my mouth.
HERMAN: I can do that.
ME: Wow, Herman, you can do it. You are pretty good at it. I didn't see
    your lips move.
HERMAN: Well, I saw yours.
ME: Ok, Herman, very funny.

One of the most important elements to master in the art of puppetry is ventiloquism. Many people want to learn how to "throw their

voice." The fact is, no one "throws" their voice. It is an illusion. Your ear does not discern where sound comes from very well. That is why you look around when you hear a siren. In ventriloquism, the sound appears to be coming from someone else. Ventriloquism is a learned skill that anyone can master. It just takes practice. The illusion is not only of your ear (what you hear), it is also an illusion of your eye (what you see). Different visual clues create this illusion. For example, we see the puppet's mouth move, not the ventriloquist's mouth. What we see and hear is different than what the reality is. The voices, mannerisms, pace, and habits that the therapist uses create the puppet character. Although ventriloquism is not mandatory in puppetry, it is fun and challenging to practice.

If other illusions are implemented in place of ventriloquism, you can still create a life-like puppet. This requires you to make the puppet mimic mannerisms, pace, and other habits of your puppet character or animal. Study an actual live animal of this type in a video or at the zoo. Study its characteristics and individualities. How does the bird move his head and take flight? Watch a snake slither or a butterfly flutter. What does it like? Dislike? What does it do? Who does it do it with? Where is it from? How old is it? What are its experiences? Practice mimicking these things with your puppet prior to using it in your office.

Figure 11.2 Understanding "Herman behavior" in the Galapagos

When the puppet's mannerisms are more exaggerated and comical, it can illustrate a point more effectively. This usually does a better job of catching a child's attention. For example, when the puppet acts surprised he dramatically jumps, engaging the child.

The word ventriloquism comes from two Latin words: *venter*, which means "stomach," and *loqui,* which means "to speak." This translates to "belly talker", which explains the technique of breathing through your diaphragm and feeling your stomach fill while you talk. This does not work with chest breathing. Take a few breaths and feel your chest and then feel your stomach. Typically we breathe through our chest. You must become a deep diaphragmatic breather to accomplish this illusion of ventriloquism. A good preliminary exercise is to suck in as much air as possible. Hold the breath for five seconds and blow out very slowly. Feel the release in your diaphragm as you blow out. Repeat this exercise five times a day.

To increase your lung capacity, hold your breath for ten seconds, and then inhale an extra burst of air. Practice this exercise five times in a row. On the sixth time, release the air with a tone. Hold the tone steady, like an emergency broadcast signal. Pinching your nose while holding the tone may assist with the tone. The longer you can hold the tone, the more successful your ventriloquism dialogue will be. This is the muscle system you use to project your voice in ventriloquism.

There are several other methods you can use to hone your ventriloquism skills. First, put your tongue behind your front teeth and say "nan." At the end of this word, hold onto the "n" sound. Your tongue will be in the proper spot in your mouth. This location is referred to as the alveolar ridge. The tongue's movement up and down on that little spot forms all of the words, sounds, syllables, and letters to make the puppet talk. "Nan" diffuses sound into the resonating cavities of your head. This positioning is key. While in this position, attention to breathing is important. In conversation, our breath comes out of our mouth. In ventriloquism, we use a dual breath stream, forcing the air up through the nasal passages so the sound comes out diffused and not direct. The sound is more difficult to track. This positioning and breathing will allow for this illusion.

An exercise for this positioning is to pop your tongue off the roof of your mouth (behind the ridge) forward and down. Flatten your tongue against the back of your upper front teeth and expel air. Experiment by shifting your tongue or expelling more or less air. Try to talk though the nasal cavity. Speak the practice word, "shay." "Shay" uses both airstreams to help you develop your tone and help you get the right voice. Feel both airways – mouth and nose – when making this sound.

In ventriloquism, there are two types of voices: near and distant. Near ventriloquism involves a puppet or other figure in front of the ventriloquist. The audience is focused on the figure. Distant ventriloquism sounds like it is coming from a distance. The audience thinks that the sound is coming from a suitcase, from behind or above the stage, etc. The distant voice is more advanced, so we will focus on the near voice in this chapter.

You will need two near voices to work with your puppet: your voice and a new voice. The new voice must be different than your own. One voice will be your own everyday voice, and the contrasting voice (the new voice) will come from the puppet.

To create the two different voices, focus on a high voice and then a low voice.

For the high voice, say "la." Continue saying "la," going up the music scale (*la la la la*) Keep going higher. Go as high as possible. Now come back down the scale until you are comfortable with this pitch and your voice is not strained – but still higher than your normal everyday voice. Say a few words in this new voice. If your voice is strained, go down a few more notes. Now, practice going further down the music scale into a deep low voice. Say "*la la la la.*" Find the lowest that you can go comfortably to accomplish the lower pitched voice. Use the same method as with the high voice and say a few words.

Choose either the higher or lower voice for your puppet to use along with your everyday voice. Now practice talking in your new voice. Practice alternating between this new voice and your everyday voice. Count to 15 seconds in the alternating voices. Your puppet should not sound like you. The new voice should have a distinct tone, pitch, and strain.

Keep in mind that the ventriloquist's mouth position has the teeth lightly together (like a smile). With your lips slightly parted, loosen your mouth. In front of a mirror, with your mouth in this position, try not to move your lips and say, "Hey, how are ya doing?"

Try saying, "Hey how are ya doing?" in the two different voices.

A pencil or popsicle stick can aid you while practicing to keep your lips slightly closed so that you are talking with your mouth in the correct position. First, in front of a mirror, place the popsicle stick or pencil lengthwise in your mouth.

Now, count to ten with the Popsicle stick inserted in your mouth. Now, count to 20 while you feel your tongue on the alveolar ridge. Try this exercise again but slide the stick out at ten.

Again, the ventriloquist's mouth position is with your teeth lightly together (like a smile). Have your lips slightly parted, loosen your mouth, and try not to move your lips. Look in a mirror. Now recite the simple letters. These include: A C D E G H I K L N O Q R S T U X Y Z.

Begin speaking in this position. Do not clench your teeth. Keep your mouth open just a little bit, like a small smile. Don't worry, this will get easier with muscle memory.

After you master the simple letters, you can advance your skill by speaking the labial letters utilizing the Maher Method (included in the online learning tools listed toward the end of the chapter). The labial letters are: B F M P V W. Although more difficult, they can be mastered with a little practice.

When these letters are spoken, your mouth must move in a certain position to make them work. These letters use sound substitutions. The tongue is used for the labial letters. The sound substitutions are as follows:

B: Say hard "D," but think "B."
For "Oh boy" say "Oh doy."
For "Beautiful" say "Deautiful."
F: Say blowing *TH* sound ("seth"), as in "Thunny."
M: Say hard "N," but think "M."
For "Emma" say "Enna."

P: Say hard "T."
Say a dish of "tickles," but think "pickles."
V: Say "thee."
Say, "thery," but think "very."
W: Say "oo," as in "roof."
Say, "ooich way do I go?"

When practicing these letters, try not to move your mouth or jaw. After you have practiced for a while, you will find that you won't need to think about the substitutions any longer. All ventriloquists eventually find their own way to substitute sounds. Substitutions take practice and experimentation. Your task is to find the best way to get the right sound for every letter and word.

Once you reach this stage, try to change your voice, and continue practicing lip control and sounds. A good exercise is to talk to your puppet in front of a mirror while looking at each other. Try keeping your expression still while making your puppet's voice expressive. Sharpen your skills by counting to 20, alternating between you and your puppet using your different voices. Rehearse the alphabet with your puppet, recite a poem, read a story, or sing a song ("99 Bottles of Beer" is a good practice song). Converse with your puppet about your day.

Creating life-like movement is another illusion necessary for successful PAPT. Where ventriloquism creates an illusion of the ear, movement creates an illusion of the eye. A therapist must learn to keep movements lively and continuous for a strong illusion of life. Jerky, bouncing movements without purpose hinder this illusion. Hone your expertise by continuous movement with your puppet while speaking and creating a rhythm.

The next lesson in movement is to practice manipulating your puppet's mouth for each syllable. The puppet's mouth should always begin a sentence in an open position and end each sentence with a closed mouth. Practice opening and closing the puppet's mouth on each syllable.

Experiment with different expressions for your puppet in a mirror. If he is surprised, he may jump up with his hands out and his mouth open. If he is sad, he may bend his head over and droop his body. He may start to cry and need to wipe his tears. If he does not agree, he may shake his head and body back and forth before turning his back on you. Happiness is portrayed with an excited up and down motion, perhaps clapping his hands using puppet rods for the arms.

When Herman the Turtle is scared, he hides in his shell. When he is loving, he leans on my shoulder. When he is angry and he is out of the "window of tolerance," I suggest that he take a few moments and go back into his shell. Herman's actions validate a child's feelings and identify their expressions and behaviors, creating a self-awareness of their body sensations that match the varying emotions they experience.

There are several very good resources to help a therapist master their puppetry techniques. One popular resource to improve your ventriloquism and puppet movement is the Maher Ventriloquism Studios in Littleton, Colorado, the headquarters for the North American Association of Ventriloquists. The Maher Method is a popular way to learn and can also be purchased on video.

Another way to master ventriloquism is a trip to the International Ventriloquism Convention and the Vent Haven Museum in Fort Mitchell, Kentucky. For several days every summer, ventriloquists world-wide attend this convention. It is worth the trip. Activities include classes, open mic performances, practice sessions, dealers' room, and entertainment. Ventriloquist Mark Wade, the host of the convention, has excellent videos for sale.

The popular ventriloquist Tom Crowl offers a course at Learnvent. com. He has several free lessons, with the option to pay for additional classes. Jeff Dunham has a course on YouTube called "How to Learn Ventriloquism."

Folkmanis Puppets Co. is a great resource to assist with this exploration of specific animals and their characteristics for puppetry. The site includes product demonstrations to view, as well as a puppet demonstration video page. This is an excellent starting place to get the feel of how to utilize puppets effectively. In addition, Folkmanis Puppets offer exceptional puppets to purchase for your playroom. Demonstration videos can be found at www.folkmanis.com/176/product-demos.htm.

Choosing the right puppet is another important element in the art of puppetry. After deciding to use PAPT in your office, the first step is to decide what kind of puppet you want to use as a prominent cotherapist puppet. Before attempting to purchase a ventriloquist puppet, a therapist or parent might first want to consider using what they have at home. A mitten is an inexpensive prototype. Sock puppets work well. Place a sock over your hand and put a rubber band between your thumb and forefingers. Decorate the sock with some eyes, a mouth and perhaps some hair.

Once you have become hooked on this ancient art, you are ready to shop for a "vent" puppet. Specialized ventriloquist puppets are available online at www.axtell.com.

Avoid buying on impulse. Let your individual interests and talents guide you. Pick a character and a voice that suits you. Opposites create a good illusion. For instance, I am high energy with a high voice, and Herman is slow moving with a low voice. Possible voice choices could be childlike, goofy, cartoon-like, sweet and innocent, macho and tough, silly, gruff, tired, baby talk, boring, a mom's or a dad's voice, or a whiny voice.

Examples of character types to consider may be a loveable puppy, a shy ostrich, a wise owl, a proper teacher, Superman, or a stunning movie star. Perhaps your coworker can be a "people" puppet. What are its likes, dislikes, favorite foods, favorite people, favorite place, or where it lives? Does it have a "catch phrase"? Achmed says, "I kill you" (https://youtu.be/GBvfiCdk-jc). Herman refers to a "turtle hurdle". How would they react in a special situation? What is their general temperament – happy, grouchy, grumpy, silly, or bossy? What gender works well with you? Do they have an accent, a southern drawl, or the whine of an irritable baby? This determination will of course assist in creating your voice. A grizzly bear profile will match the voice and will sound deep and gruff. A grandmother can have a sweet demeanor and that characteristic corresponding voice.

Puppets come with a wide choice of options. I believe that soft puppets, as opposed to the hard puppets, fare better in a playroom. Sometimes people, especially children, are afraid of the hard-cased puppets.

Puppets are available with levers for moving eyes from side to side, moving eyebrows up and down, moving tongues, blinking eyes, wiggling noses, spinning heads, and even spitting. Any of these options will enhance the lifelike personalities of your puppet.

Once you have chosen a puppet and are fairly proficient in ventriloquism and puppet movements, record a video of yourself talking with your puppet, alternating between voices. Play it back to hear the differences. To gain confidence, rehearse the various voices and movement activities before telling a story with your puppet in a mirror.

There are a few things to consider before putting your cotherapist puppet to work in your playroom:

- Remember to keep the puppet alive.
- Have the puppet on your hand before you introduce it to a child.
- Move the puppet's mouth in time to the syllables. Move the mouth for every syllable. Tap on your leg to practice the rhythm.
- Don't let the puppet snap or bite air. Open and close its mouth gently.
- Keep its head up, staring and looking around.
- How you hold a puppet is important. Hold it at your eye level so you can talk to it face-to-face.
- Have the puppet look away, shake its head, and look back again.
- Hold onto its feet or rest the puppet on a stool so it is not hanging on your hand.
- Cock its head. Shake its head in frustration.
- Have it jump when it is excited.
- Create habits for your puppet.
- And finally, never forget to fully involve your client.

Have fun, be adaptable, safe, empathetic, "real," creative, challenging, and entertaining. Remember, mistakes are okay. And be careful not to share the magic technique – it takes the fun out of it.

Termination is an essential stage of the therapeutic process, and it is critical to properly conduct the closure of the puppet session. This can be accomplished in numerous ways. It is important to never take your hand out of the puppet in view of children. I have children close the curtain on my puppet stage. Herman goes into his shell and back to his chair after he says his goodbyes.

Practice makes perfect with PAPT. Your cotherapist puppet is intrinsic to the therapeutic relationship. Make this fantasy appear to be a reality. A realistic puppet can quickly break down barriers between a therapist and a child. Children will always listen to Herman.

12 Puppets Worldwide

One might think that most of the world is familiar with puppets in some form, but my experiences have been different. Many of the children I have worked with in my travels have never experienced puppets before. I have learned firsthand how easily puppets can create a connection and bridge between totally different cultures. This chapter shares those extraordinary connections.

When I traveled from the Old City of Jerusalem, where Palestinian boys giggled at meeting a monkey puppet, to the villages of Cameroon, Africa, and Haiti, children met puppets for the first time with surprise and delight. I once read that smiling is a truly universal language. After watching children in Israel and Africa interact with puppets, I would say that puppets and puppet play serves the same purpose. Play is the language of childhood. Through play, children are able to understand each other and make sense of the world around them. Therapeutically, educationally, and spiritually, puppets communicate a smiling connection amongst children across the globe.

I have always enjoyed play, toys, and stuffed animals. As I began studying for my Master's in Social Work, I immediately focused in on play therapy. This seemed to be a reflection of my passion for working with children and mental health. My undergraduate degree was in therapeutic recreation, and as I pursued my education, I realized that healing and play are intertwined. My research topic was obvious – puppets in play therapy.

I began searching for a helper in my research project and preferred the larger puppets. I chose a bear ventriloquist puppet whom I named Bear-niece to assist with my research, and the story of this book began. After working with Bear-niece for a time, I learned about the Annual International Ventriloquist Convention in Kentucky, booked a ticket, and became immersed in puppetry. A full schedule of events is included at this convention including presentations, information and classes. In the dealers' room, I noticed a turtle on the shelf. His eyes

Figure 12.1 Bear-niece, Herman, and me

spoke to me, and I could not leave without him. My daughter helped name him Herman, and he is now a major character in my playroom, presentations, book, and life.

As you already know, Herman is my cotherapist puppet who is a "So-Shell worker" and a member of the British Columbia Association for So-Shell Workers. His certificate of merit hangs in my office along with Bear-niece's certificate and they, along with the Family Bearapist, Peter the Pooper, Bryan the Brain, and Betsy and Lucy, my service dogs, are part of the team that is well known in my practice. This is the team that children and parents refer to when they come to "Herman's House."

My first foray into international PAPT began in Haiti in 2010. On January 20 of that year, a 7.0 magnitude earthquake hit and devastated

Haiti. An estimated three million people were affected by the quake, nearly one third of the country's total population. Of these, over one million were left homeless in the immediate aftermath. In devastated urban areas, the displaced were forced to gather in ramshackle temporary cities patched together with scrounged materials and donated tents. The Haitian Government's official death toll was more than 300,000. International aid groups reported that tens of thousands of children were newly orphaned. There were so many that Haitian officials wouldn't even venture a number. As one of the world's poorest countries, Haiti was awash in trauma. The United Nations Children's Fund estimated that 380,000 children lived in orphanages or group homes after the deadly event.

When I saw the tragic pictures of stunned, newly orphaned children on the news from the comfort of my Canadian home, I knew that my puppets and I would go and help. I packed an assortment of puppets in my luggage before I set off to assist, including a smaller travelling version of Herman and crafts to decorate the puppets.

The earthquake had crippled the main airport, most of the ports, and almost all the paved roads, making it difficult for relief efforts to reach the survivors. I arrived alone in Port-au-Prince with massive amounts of luggage for my work. The airport had closed shortly after I arrived, and I was standing in isolation waiting for a prearranged ride that never appeared. The scene was chaotic and frightening. Remembering the recent reports of tourist kidnappings, I felt very white and very vulnerable.

Fearful and unsure what to do, I took Herman out of my bag and began chatting with him about the situation. A family approached and the children began staring at us while conversing in Creole, not knowing what to think. They began to laugh. Within a short period of time, more children and their parents began surrounding me. Everyone was laughing. I pulled out several of my homemade puppets and passed them around. Before I knew it, I had a shield of laughing families enclosed around my bags and me to keep me safe until my ride appeared. Puppets had kept me safe, made the Haitians happy, and helped me nurture new friends in the country. My puppets saved the day.

While sitting outside the closed airport on my return to Canada, I became frightened again. I found two Haitian children who were sitting on the steps nearby, pulled two puppets from my pack, and gave them to the children. Parents were enjoying these puppets as well, and encouraged friends to join us. Not long after the arrival of the puppets, I was surrounded by numerous families with many children feeling safe, laughing, and playing with puppets. These puppets saved the day once more.

My puppets and I spent six weeks on the island of Haiti. I gave away all 1,000 puppets, arts and craft supplies, and trauma books, which totaled 200 pounds of luggage. The trauma puppet program was an incredible success; the magical puppets were a lifeline for a smile, a laugh, a momentary release from the chaos and loss that surrounded everybody in Haiti.

In Haiti, I was looking for a translator and met Marjorie Salvodon at HODR. It is now named All Hands and Hearts and is a nonprofit organization that assists with worldwide disasters by removing debris before volunteers from Habitat for Humanity come and rebuild. Marjorie, a native Haitian, had recently moved to Boston. She returned to the disaster and offered to help me with my trauma program. We visited numerous orphanages and she helped to translate and to organize the project at the different sites. The puppet program was a success for her as well. She adopted one of the babies from the orphanage, who is presently thriving in Boston.

We sent the following "Helping Herman Report" to the directors at All Hands and Hearts for their newsletter. They publish what they have accomplished in Haiti and in other volunteer projects around the world, for both volunteers and sponsors. If you would like to donate to this agency, please refer to their site at www.allhandsandhearts.org.

Figure 12.2 A village of puppets

Helping Herman Report

We used the *Brave Bart* children's book, written by Caroline Sheppard (1998), during the HODR visit to the orphanage in Léogâne, Haiti. This story was adapted from Sheppard by Cheryl Hulburd, who also adapted the illustrations by John Manikoff. Originally, Brave Bart was a cat, in this version he is a turtle – of course! The story book is called *Helping Herman*. This book has been used with therapists and counselors who work with children on issues related to trauma. The version used at the orphanage was translated into Creole by three local and international volunteers.

The story's content describes an unnamed terrible thing that happens to Bart, the turtle protagonist. Throughout the telling of Bart's story, which chronicles his different reactions to the terrible thing, the readers watch him befriend another (bigger) turtle named Helping Herman, who helps him to take care of himself, feel good about himself, play with his friends once more, and enjoy the sea as he once did, before the terrible thing befell Bart.

This is a story of hope and healing. It is also universal; the terrible thing is never identified except for the fact that it is a "bad, sad, and scary" thing. This helps many children to be able to relate to Bart and his story, and they are able to imagine their own terrible thing as something that may have happened to Bart.

The children listened to the story and looked at the gorgeous illustrations with rapt attention. They asked questions like, "What happened to Bart?" Although we did not follow the original curriculum developed by the trauma therapists, we had successful discussions with the children about what terrible thing might have happened to Bart.

If the first part of this pedagogical tool reinforces empathy and develops listening skills, the second part focuses on action and is directed to each individual child present. In the second part of the program, children choose three pieces from a variety of materials (fabric, fur, colored string, sequins, ribbon, foam shapes, googly eyes, etc.) to decorate their hand-held puppets. In the story, one of the things that Helping Herman tells Bart to do is "find someone to talk with." In this activity, children are told that the puppets are their friends, and that they can talk to them.

The children at the orphanage loved hearing Bart's story, and they enjoyed making a new puppet friend who they could also decorate as they chose. Although we did not complete the full program at the orphanage, the children were very interested in the story and in having a new friend. When fully executed, this program empowers children to deal with past hurts and to heal themselves.

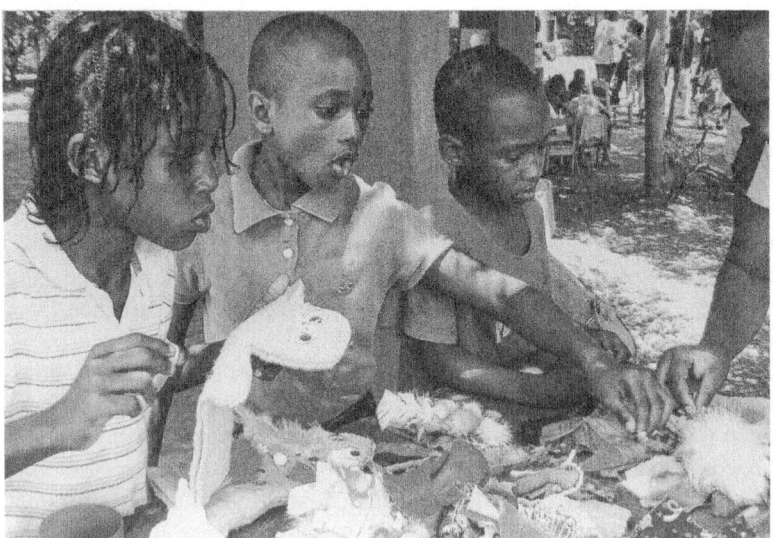

Figure 12.3 WOW!

Cheryl is leaving the *Brave Bart* program with All Hands and Hearts. This program includes process questions to be used with individual children and discussion topic questions for groups of children. The program comes with the English version of the story as well as the Creole one.

We believe that Brave Bart (or Kiki Kouraje, as the protagonist is called in the Creole version) is a useful and powerful tool to use with children in the aftermath of any traumatic incident. We hope that many Haitian children will have the opportunity to meet Bart and Herman/ Kiki Kouraje and to heal from their trauma.

After Marjorie traveled home to Boston, Herman and I hired a moped and a translator so we could visit other orphanages and villages around the country as a freelance volunteer therapist similar to a Non-Governmental Organization (NGO). The ladies referred to Herman as an NGI, nonprofit individual!

PAPT and New Lands

As I was freelancing in Haiti, I learned that Cameroon needed help with domestic violence programming and within months of my return from Haiti, I was back on a plane headed for Cameroon. I met up with Celeste Youonzo at CEFASE, an NGO. Celeste is the director and translator for CEFASE. We rode out via moped to remote villages outside the city of Yaoundé. We hiked from village to village for three weeks teaching men, women, and children about domestic violence. I set up several safe homes in the nearby villages and spent a great deal of time with puppets and children. I used the puppets to role model domestic violence emergencies, learn about feelings, and provide tools for the caregivers to help with children's trauma from violence. The families in Cameroon where I visited seemed to be plagued with violence from men to women, women to children, and children to animals. Oppression was discussed, as well as empathy. Again, the puppets and I were well received, and I believe we planted a seed in the villages regarding abstinence from violence.

Several year later, I chose to travel to Ecuador for an extended holiday. Because I had such moving experiences in Africa, I decided to take sewn puppets, supplies to decorate them, and materials for my trauma program into a jungle village of the Amazon that I had always dreamed of visiting. Not sure what I would find, I emerged from a fishing boat that I had hired onto the shore of a remote village. Once again, I was the only North American in a sea of curious Ecuadorian faces.

After my past experiences, I knew exactly what to do. I pulled out my trusted turtle, Herman, and several homemade puppets to distribute.

Figure 12.4 Santa Domingo de la Tsachila Village, Ecuador

I was readily accepted into this village with hugs, giggles, and squeals of delight. To my surprise, the village did not have any major trauma or domestic violence issues. The children were playing outside, unplugged from electronics. As my trauma program was not needed, I began playing with the children with no agenda in mind. The children put the puppets on their heads as hats. I soon realized that these children had never seen puppets and began to teach them how to use their new friends by inserting their hand in the bottom sleeve. We used a table on its side for the puppet stage, and I was thoroughly entertained with shows and songs during my visit. Although I achieved none of my therapeutic mental health goals to speak of, I was received as a family member by the end of my stay. The connection of puppets is powerful. I now revisit this village often. The puppets created a bond that has lasted for years and has certainly improved my mental health due to the hospitality and warm welcome I found.

Plans for a new trip to Indonesia set the puppet production in motion once again. I researched and found an orphanage in Bali that seemed like a good fit with Herman. The orphanage was overcrowded and provisions were low; however, there were many volunteers to help educate the children. One little girl approached me asking me what was in my travel bags. I pulled out Herman and the children came running to meet him. The children were thrilled to partake in this puppet program. They listened intently to the story book, *Helping Herman*, and then were able to relate their own terrible experiences with the messages of Herman's "bad, sad, and scary thing that happened." The opportunity to evoke just a smile from an orphan is magnificent. A puppet totally enhances these smiles and enriches their lives.

This puppet scenario happens whenever and wherever I travel with Herman. Now, I never leave my trusted companion behind.

As I think about my travels with puppets I am honored, blessed, and grateful for how my puppets have allowed me to befriend people, especially children, around the world. My first stop in Israel was in the Old City of Jerusalem. As I am a Jew, the Palestinians seemed to be reluctant to engage with me. However, when I pulled out my puppets, young Palestinian boys who were playing in the streets approached me. Puppets once again bridged the gap as we smiled and played together.

PAPT is implementable worldwide. The language of puppetry strikes a universal chord, which touches the hearts of audiences around the globe. The healing effects of this modality reach all cultures, with minor adaptations focused on the individual sensitivities for each arena of tradition. Practices may vary with subtle intricacies for any country or group that possesses unique ways of life and customs.

PAPT, as new as it is, has expanded in various cultures with new ideas in different settings around the globe. The story book *Helping Herman* has been translated into other languages and distributed worldwide to many orphanages. As *Helping Herman* deals with general trauma, it can easily be implemented for any trauma that requires healing.

The Haitian disaster taught me a great deal. I experienced camaraderie among the victims, the drive to survive, and gratitude for the safe, protected place that I call home. I try to adhere to the quote, "May we find our life so precious that we cannot but share it with another" (Stern, 1999).

In Indonesian orphanages, Herman and I discovered not only that children of all countries relate in a universally positive way to puppets, but also that puppets can assist universally in the trauma of loss.

Cameroon, Africa, presented a different challenge. There, we learned about the nuances of violent culture and the steps necessary to achieve change for domestic violence. Love and laughter are the antidote for trauma around the globe.

Ecuador is an amazing country that offers exciting travel. The villagers I met were some of the warmest people in the world. Herman and I found a safe haven to visit and our new extended family rejuvenates us to continue our PAPT journey.

A recent trip involved a volunteer position at C.A.R.E. (Centre for Animal Rehabilitation and Education) Baboon Sanctuary in South

Figure 12.5 Herman steals the show

Figure 12.6 South African workshop at C.A.R.E. – baboons are our friends

Africa. The agenda for this organization was conservation and education for the local children. After viewing educational information and knowing from my travelling experiences the response of children to puppets, I suggested we implement a puppet show about poaching and its implications. A baboon stuffed animal was purchased and transformed into a puppet to demonstrate how C.A.R.E. helps the baboons.

Travel is a passion for me that allows a new way of thinking, understanding, and believing. It creates new friendships and helps Herman and me to grow into more skilled helpers. Travel has enhanced my spirituality, health, and relationships. Each culture and setting have their own individual hurdles to overcome. Puppets are effective tools to teach, heal, entertain, and love with no language barriers. If the universal language of PAPT is so effective, why not use puppets for all the issues directed at children worldwide?

13 Ethical Concerns

The modality of play therapy addresses professional concerns that arise in this modern age of litigation and awareness. In this chapter, these concerns within PAPT are discussed. As mental health professionals, and those of us who work in a professional capacity with children, we need to recognize the complex nature of ethical guidelines by which we practice/work. Understanding and consideration of ethical principles and standards guides the process of our ethical decision-making choices. Ethical conflicts require both documentation and consultation. Because of the changing laws governing children, and children's rights, one must remain cognizant of the law and ethics concerning practice in your area.

Professional responsibility clearly emphasizes working within our scope of practice, being aware of our own competency, professional limits, and training. Do no harm is inclusive in every ethics code. PAPT is no different. Several ethical concerns to consider with puppets are the professional responsibility regarding:

1. Confidentiality.
2. Recognizing repetitive and aggressive play in your playroom while using puppets.
3. The ethical dilemma of touching.
4. Competence in the realm of abuse disclosure, including familiarity with litigation.
5. Cultural sensitivity.

Confidentiality

Clarification of informed consent and confidentiality have guidelines in each state and province. Children's confidentiality must be honored under the limits of the law. If child abuse is involved, reporting is mandated no matter how information is obtained in the playroom.

Children must have a safe place to share. Confidentiality must not be overlooked during the play aspect of puppetry. This is especially true with high-conflict divorce.

It is important to note that while assessing a child, caution is advised. A child can use puppet play to avoid expressing feelings, thoughts, and issues relating to their traumatic experiences. Children may resist involvement in any of the play. The therapist must recognize this and address the situation with expertise or consultation. When this occurs it may be an indication that they are facing their trauma too soon, too intensely, or avoiding. This may affect the therapy and/or assessment. Attention to timing is vital. In my experience, children who avoid are not ready to address issues. Herman, my cotherapist puppet, reflects the play with patience and allows the child to proceed at their own pace without rushing the process.

Aggression in the Playroom

Another practice concern addresses aggression in the playroom. Children may hit for various reasons. They may be reenacting aggression in their lives, performing superhero themes, or acting in a cathartic manner. It is beneficial to recognize and understand aggressive tendencies and their meanings as well as the therapeutic value of aggressive behavior of each child within PAPT

Depending on the child's development, it is not uncommon for young children to hit other puppets when they are introduced to this activity. I encourage children to learn puppet manipulation. If the puppet's hands or mouth are movable, I show the child how to hold the puppet erect and how to move its mouth when speaking. With practice, the child gains confidence in the puppet experience and this type of aggressive play behavior is diminished.

Repetitive symbolic play is a therapeutic process. Repetitive symbolic play with puppets is purposeful and therapeutic in that it allows children to actively engage with past emotional experiences while altering these outcomes through play (Findling et al., 2006). Landreth (2002) described repetitive play as repeated engagement with either the same toys and/or play activities. Repetitive play behavior is understood as an expression of the trauma that is being repeatedly communicated in the present with the same theme. These are not stagnant, nonpurposeful, repeated reenactments evident in traumatic play, but rather dynamic attempts at meaning making and problem solving (Findling et al., 2006).

A therapist may capitalize on the bonding experience or address the contraindication of repetitive aggressive thematic trauma play with the use of puppets.

When children were surveyed, the research concluded that "rough and tumble play" mostly represents a pleasurable way to connect. "The interview data reveals how up to 85% of play fighting partners are friends. The vast majority of children grasp the essential difference between rough-and-tumble play and real aggressive conflict. By age 10 about 96% of children are able distinguish between play fighting and real fighting" (Smith et al., 2004).

Cathartic behavior linked with the expression of aggression has long been debated within the therapeutic community. Irwin and Shapiro (1975) maintained that cathartic relief helped children vent their anger thereby benefiting from this type of play. Other scholars have also defended this hypothesis and claimed that aggression release can benefit and improve one's emotional state. Other researchers have challenged this theory. Geen and Quanty (1977) concluded that venting anger does not reduce aggression and it perhaps can result in additional aggression. Warren and Kurlychek (1981) asserted that once children learn that aggressive behavior is acceptable and rewarding, they are more likely to choose it in the future. Bushman (2002) suggested that venting is practicing how to behave aggressively and contended that the cathartic behavior does not reduce aggression nor reduce negative affect. Aggressive traumatic puppet play is another area of competence practice. The dilemma concerning aggression and puppet play weapons are reoccurring themes in PAPT. Drewes responds, "Each child has a unique story with a unique treatment approach. In light of this research, it is important to monitor and perhaps intervene with the puppets to help reduce anger" (Drewes, 2008, pp. 52–65).

Touch

Touch is an ethical dilemma in the playroom. According to Barnard and Brazelton (1990), "Touch functions on many levels of adaptation, first to make survival possible, and then to make life meaningful" (p. 561). Understanding the neurobiology of touch as related to emotional, cognitive, physical, and interpersonal development has revealed the crucial importance of touch from birth and throughout the life span (McGlone, Wessberg, & Olausson, 2014). We have long known that without certain types of nurturing touch, contact that is beyond feeding and basic needs, a child will not thrive and may even die (Spitz & Wolf, 1946). Those who work with children understand that touch is essential for children's healthy growth and development and is not precluded when used as a therapeutic intervention.

When a child experiences touch from a caring and safe caregiver, many things happen to promote healthy growth. Children develop a sense of self and the ability to relate well to others. They learn to regulate affect and behavior and develop a positive self-esteem.

Research indicates that touch is essential in forming secure attachment between the parent and the child, fostering physiological development, reducing the effect of stress on an infant, and promoting positive body image (Booth & Jernberg, 2010). Touch is essential to promote growth and provide healing. When misused, it can impede healthy development and cause harm. In addition to the child's reaction to touch, other distinctions include whether the touch is initiated by the child or the therapist, and ultimately whether the touch is therapeutic or in some cases even harmful (Courtney & Siu, 2018). Because touch is a complex, powerful form of communication, play therapists must carefully evaluate and understand their own motivations for using or not using touch, and whether or not this action meets the needs of the child.

Play therapists need to be aware that touch is a very sensitive topic today. Organizations have policies and procedures in place addressing the use of touch. Play therapists should be aware that different cultures have distinct values and meanings to touch. It is imperative to understand how touch is expressed within each child's culture. The therapist must be prepared to manage any touching that occurs and also the perception of that touch by the child and the child's caretakers.

> Research indicates that appropriate touch can be important in the treatment of trauma. A play therapist is ever vigilant not to re-traumatize a child.
>
> The ethical dilemma of touch is considered with varying opinions and responses. Hence, this issue can lead to a serious allegation in fluctuating contexts. A familiar child who has recently been sexually abused can become re-traumatized; A child who needs nurturance can interpret all types of touch as appropriate attention; Touch can influence trust issues, etc., all need reflection. The most recent research claims that 70% of respondents in the touch study indicated that they were concerned or had mixed reactions regarding professional liability related to touch in sessions, but the majority indicated that they did indeed touch their child clients.
>
> (Courtney & Siu, 2018, p. 99)

Brody (1997) introduced developmental play therapy, a therapeutic approach that also addresses the attachment theory. This therapy emphasizes the use of physical contact. Her theory rests on the key point that touch can help foster secure attachment with children (Brody, 1997).

Figure 13.1 Safe hug

The dilemma continues of whether or not to touch. However, with PAPT the puppets do the hugging and touching. The children love to be hugged by their favorite puppet.

The resolution is easy, the answer is PAPT.

Abuse Disclosure

One area of touch that needs to be discussed is the subject of abuse disclosure. Touch is a trigger for disclosure. Please do not attempt to pursue this disclosure without appropriate expertise. Learn the laws in your area regarding testimony if disclosure occurs. Please understand the various videotaping legalities and issues in your area.

Professional responsibility with regard to competence also must be acknowledged in the treatment of EMDR. Chapter 14 introduces PAPT with eye-movement desensitization and reprocessing. This modality requires basic training along with supervision.

Cultural Sensitivity

More so than ever, cultural sensitivity is at the forefront of our social paradigm and PAPT is no exception. Therapists need to be extra sensitive to this issue. Being culturally sensitive with puppets may sound straight forward, but is it? It is imperative to study the culture, the meanings in language, and the values and beliefs in any diverse population. Individual treatment is paramount for each child during puppet-assisted play therapy.

"Responsibility to Society" speaks to the need to respect and be sensitive to diversity – cultural, religious, racial, etc. It is therefore advisable to incorporate this diversity in your puppet repertoire in the playroom. Ethnic dolls, costumes, and indigenous animals are appropriate.

Recently, while in South Africa, I created a puppet show for C.A.R.E. and the local children to teach about poaching. I purchased new stuffed animals to convert into puppets for the show; a baboon mom, a baby baboon, and a male person puppet to be the poacher. Being in Africa and having a black audience, I automatically picked out a black male puppet. When I arrived at C.A.R.E., the South African director suggested that I not use the black male due to the implication that all poachers are black. I never thought twice about the message until it was brought to my attention! Awareness of local implications and customs is crucial. It is helpful to learn about the culture from books, formal educational sources and, if possible, the local native population.

The selection of animal puppets also requires consideration. For example, in Haiti cats are considered part of the everyday diet. Puppets need to be modified depending on the culture. Brave Bart was a cat in the original publication, but when I was in Haiti I changed the cat character into a turtle because of this cultural difference. In India, a cow is sacred and perhaps should not be part of a puppet show. The raven in American Native culture is significantly different than an eagle in the United States. Cultural sensitivity can make or break a therapeutic relationship, and this relationship directly impacts the healing process.

In summary, no therapeutic modality is applicable to or beneficial for everyone. Different techniques and approaches within the PAPT structure are advantageous when working with clients. Ethical situations are challenging. These may occur in any treatment scenario such as cultural settings, during periods of grief, child–parent relationships, or the aftermath of trauma. Ethical challenges require supervision or consultation and documentation. It would behoove play therapists to address the unique ethical and legal issues found in play therapy.

14 PAPT and EMDR

Disclaimer: The implementation of EMDR practice without comprehensive training is unethical. Hence, not all components of the EMDR protocol will be elaborated on in this section. Preliminary steps and exercises (phases one to three) used for planning, preparation, and assessment of EMDR processing with children will be inclusive. Reprocessing steps (phases four to eight) will be only briefly detailed.

Puppet-assisted play therapy and eye-movement desensitization and reprocessing (EMDR) are complementary. EMDR is an evidence-based therapeutic approach that processes traumatic memory to reset the brain. In *Eye Movement Desensitization and Reprocessing: Basic Principles, Protocols and Procedures*, Shapiro (2001) contended that traumatic memory consists of maladaptive material with negative self-representations resulting from traumatic experiences. The process of reset occurs when the memory is digested, along with the stuck feelings, thoughts, and body sensations intrinsic to the trauma.

The brain's innate information processing system involves the concept of memory networks. A memory network represents an associated system of information (Shapiro, 2001). Traumatic experiences are held in this memory system in the form of thoughts, feelings, and sensations. PAPT is an engaging, playful, and healing way to complement EMDR while addressing these memory systems.

EMDR is divided into eight phases:

1. Client history and treatment planning;
2. Preparation;
3. Assessment;
4. Desensitization/reprocessing;
5. Installation;
6. Body scan;
7. Closure; and
8. Reevaluation.

As mentioned earlier, puppets provide safety in the therapeutic process by acting as a once-removed or twice-removed medium. Safety is essential for all phases of EMDR and other therapies. If children do not feel safe they may not engage, share, confide, or even play. In EMDR, retraumatization can occur if the protocol is not adhered to. The therapist must ensure that children can tolerate the feelings, thoughts, and sensations of the scary or painful memory that they revisit in the processing phase of EMDR.

Puppets are an excellent medium to learn about the child's story. Children sometimes want to hide in order to feel safe, and hiding behind the puppet stage with their favorite puppets may enable the child to better disclose and process. The puppets can be placed on an easily accessible shelf during therapy to help support and comfort the children. Gary Landreth (Bratton et al., 2006) suggested the therapist continue talking through this hiding period to let the child know that "you are here, that you understand, and that you care" (p. 16).

The first phase of EMDR, client history and treatment planning, entails the evaluation of the child's functioning, symptoms, behaviors, and attitudes. These elements need to be addressed during the development of an individualized, detailed treatment plan. The child's ability to withstand intense emotion must also be explored.

After a therapist obtains a detailed history from the child's caretakers, the therapist does the same with the child. The "Peek a Boo" puppet technique can assist with coaxing the child into the therapist's playroom and help begin the play. The game can expand further into a variation of this technique if the child is shy and timid or does not want to engage in the playroom (see Chapter 7).

The Bird-day Party technique and the geno-puppet-o-gram (see Figure 6.1, page 45), both mentioned earlier, or an individual puppet show that illustrates the presenting problems experienced by the child, can all be used for the treatment planning phase with the child. I use my Peter the Pooper puppet when discovering the children's presenting problems. Peter, a poop puppet, asks the children what is poopy in their lives. The children laugh and giggle at Peter, especially when he farts. They are quickly absorbed in this play, which accelerates their involvement and participation in their treatment process.

Phase one begins with the child's history and treatment planning and the process of identifying the child's targets. The targets are the memories that are keeping the child from optimal mental health. Additional targets will continue to be discovered throughout the EMDR process. At times, it is difficult for children to discuss or even demonstrate through play their disturbing experiences and memories. When children identify a difficult memory, I often shower them

Figure 14.1 Peter the Pooper puppet (Peter the Pooper puppet can be purchased at www.ferniecounselling.ca)

with "magic dust" from a sorcerer's or wizard's magic wand. Magical moments in therapy are powerful, and glitter symbolizes magic in my playroom. Invisible dust is also acceptable. Such magical and creative thinking can expand beyond the playroom toys and puppets to enhance communication.

After the child identifies the target memories, they can be saved in a homemade customized puppet, which holds them until we are ready to address and process them. Feelings buttons made from foam circles inserted in the homemade turtle puppets (see Chapter 7) can be turned into memory buttons. These memory buttons can be held by any puppet that the child chooses. Felt or paper memories can be attached with Velcro to any puppet or the puppet's prop. My rabbit puppet appears out of a magic hat, which is a popular place to store memories. The child may also attach the memories to the arms of an octopus which holds them safe until needed. Numerous puppets can be used for these stored memories. These puppets can be purchased from www.ferniecounselling.ca (see Appendix B).

Therapists need to be cognizant of correct timing when revisiting traumatic memories. Expertise is needed to understand and address their window of tolerance, as well as their ability to remain in dual awareness. A detailed explanation of identifying additional targets is mentioned later in the chapter.

An effective medium used to learn about a child's stories for EMDR is a sand tray. Ana Gomez (2013), a leading expert in the use of EMDR with children, explained this process in her book, *EMDR Therapy and Adjunct Approaches with Children*. If sand tray therapy is used to identify memories or targets, puppets can be utilized afterwards in order to create an intermediate step for better titration of the trauma memory before processing. The memories contained in the sand can be titrated one step further with puppet involvement by partly owning or wearing (on a hand) the trauma experience before directly revisiting the experience. The child may feel additional safety with the fact that the cotherapist puppet is there to help them through this process. For increased safety, they can choose a puppet that they are comfortable with to support them through their processing phase.

The second phase of EMDR is the preparation phase. It offers multiple opportunities to effectively utilize PAPT. This phase involves "establishing a therapeutic alliance, explaining the EMDR process and its effects, addressing the child's concerns and initiating relaxation and safety procedures" (Shapiro, 2001, p. 71). The preparation phase prepares the child for both assessing and processing the memories. Once a child is familiar with the protocol, they can implement all they have learned during the next phases. After establishing the therapeutic alliance, the therapist explains EMDR to the child with a basic neurobiology lesson so they can understand how the brain and memories work. Children are then taught calming exercises. They learn about the window of tolerance, dissociation, and behavior. They are taught about emotions, body sensations, and cognitions relating to traumatic memory. Puppets aid in these lessons.

Establishing an effective therapeutic alliance is automatic with Herman the Turtle. Any cotherapist puppet will substantially help with the success of the second phase. The preparation, phase two, also involves the explanation of change.

Puppets can be used to illustrate this change. An impressive Monarch Life Cycle puppet can be used to illustrate the change from caterpillar, to chrysalis, to an adult monarch butterfly. Children love playing with this majestic puppet and learn about the stages of change and transformation. Other puppets such as the frog's life cycle and lady bug's life cycle portray the same change. This metaphorical introduction of EMDR can be useful in this second phase. Gary Landreth (Bratton et al., 2006) provides a short story about the struggles, development, and change of butterflies in his Child Parent Relationship Therapy manual that can be used in conjunction with the puppet. These puppets can be purchased at www.ferniecounselling.ca (see Appendix B).

Explaining the EMDR process through brain education is helpful. I have developed a brain puppet for this function. A good time to introduce Bryan the Brain is when the child is learning about the brain, its integration, and EMDR. Bryan talks to both the child and to Herman, my cotherapist puppet.

Bryan the Brain explains to the child how he works by illustrating his upper brain, lower brain, right hemisphere, and left hemisphere, and demonstrates how integration works. He explains that we hold memories in our thoughts, emotions, and body sensations. Bryan encourages the child to share information, asks the child or the child's brain puppet if they have any questions, and asks if they would be interested in working through their "bad, sad, and scary thing that happened to them" (Sheppard, 1998, p. 1) with the puppets. Bryan is available for purchase at www.ferniecounselling.ca (see Appendix B).

In this phase, the child's ability to endure negative and positive emotions must be increased. This is referred to as affect tolerance. If a child leaves the window of tolerance, they will become either hypoaroused or hyperaroused. Various puppets can demonstrate hyperarousal, such as an angry dragon, T-Rex, wolf, badger, or tiger. Oaklander (1978) describes how one learns much about a child through the puppet they pick, and provides an example of a client who chooses a tiger. The child begins his interaction by explaining, "I am fierce, everyone is afraid of me! I bite people who come near me" (Oaklander, 1978, p. 105). Children illustrate hypoarousal by selecting puppets that shut down, hide, or dissociate, such as a clam, baby kangaroo, june bug, ostrich, or snail. A marvelous selection of puppets that enrich this concept are available such as: a bear in a tree stump, a chipmunk in a watermelon, a giant clam, a hermit crab, a dinosaur in an egg, a dragon in a turret, a rabbit in a hat, a mouse in a pumpkin, a racoon in a garbage can, a rat in a tin can and of course numerous tortoises and turtles (see Appendix B).

After an explanation of dissociation, or shutting down, I ask children to show me if and how much they dissociate. Jim Knipe developed a technique called *Back of the Head*, whereby clients show how far away they are from "losing a felt sense of the reality and safety of the present situation." They do this by moving their hands close to or far from their head. This motion measures the intensity of dissociation or shutting down and can lead to "drifting into de-realization" during the processing phase. This procedure allows both the client and therapist to monitor and maintain the "dual attention aspect of successful trauma processing" (Knipe, as cited in Luber, 2010, p. 233).

Dual attention describes attending to the present and past trauma time simultaneously. I explain this concept utilizing the metaphor of a snail that is open or closed (in or out of his shell), a clam, rabbit in a hat, or a puppet crab that is hiding as opposed to the crab that crawls here beside me. Of course, one can't forget a turtle puppet. A turtle can demonstrate this dual attention aspect with his head out, holding dual attention, as opposed to being in his shell, representing dissociation and floating away from the here and now. In *Shelly's Shell*, Steffy (2010) explains that her turtle puppet's shell "protects her from danger" (p. 7).

During the second phase of EMDR, it is also useful to explain survival strategies/defense mechanisms to children. Children may develop these strategies when they are young in a threatening situation to stay safe. They may continue to use them in later life, which hinders their functioning. It is important for children to learn about these patterns of behavior. Using puppets that have similar characteristics that match their behavior patterns can help their awareness. For example, a clown puppet can receive laughs for attention and be a positive asset. Utilizing similar silly behavior in a structured environment such as a classroom will hinder performance. Kaduson and Schaefer (1997) stated that "a puppet can be devised to represent, introduce, and describe themselves, their concerns, and desires" (p. 192).

For example, children in the midst of a domestic violence situation will learn quickly that they will be safer if they move away from the scene. They learn to "go into their shell," metaphorically speaking, to find comfort and safety. They may create this pattern as a go-to behavior when they are in danger. This reaction may be amplified in any or all stressful situations that they experience. Assertive behavior is not in their repertoire of options when addressing current or future life situations. People and animals protect themselves in different ways. By using puppets to learn and identify these strategies, children are better able to understand and own these behaviors from a safe distance.

Children must learn how to calm themselves prior to revisiting unpleasant or painful memories. Fortunately, there are several PAPT techniques that work well to accomplish this. One is referred to as ego state change, an essential skill of EMDR in the preparation phase. Therapists use ego state change to teach relaxation and safety, both of which are required for the processing stage.

Children practice creating a "safe place" where they can imagine being in a safe place of their choosing. This is an ego state change skill that converts the threatening state to the calm state. Bibliotherapy, mentioned earlier in Chapter 8, also provides relaxing exercises that help calm children by using PAPT. Calming exercises can be achieved by replicating characters in the following books. *The Calm Cat* by Williams and O'Quinn Burke (2007), *Peaceful Piggy Meditation* by MacLean (2004), and *Moody Cow Meditates* by MacLean (2009) are just a few of the many resources that assist with calming.

A heart is one popular puppet assistant that I use when a child feels alone, powerless, and difficult to calm. The heart puppet is used in conjunction with *The Invisible String* by Patrice Karst (2000). I read the story, and the heart puppet describes how we are all connected together by its invisible string. I elaborate by explaining that their caregiver or their puppet is with them everywhere they go, always connected to them by the invisible string of love.

There are other ways to introduce the concept of ego state change using PAPT. In my office, Herman asks if the child will join him on a guided visualization trip to the ocean to come swim with him and his other turtle friends (refer to Chapter 8 for this script). This exercise works well in introducing the intentional creation of a calm state. This particular ego state change relaxation exercise is a favorite of mine. I teach this to parents so they can continue using this calming technique at home. They may choose a different puppet from their own toy box to create unique guided imagery.

Magic can also be a calming force for children to help them develop and revisit their "happy place" feelings. Using magic enhances children's belief that they have power over natural forces, or that they possess the qualities that help them heal. Well known superheroes are represented in my cache of puppets. PAPT is tailor-made for the use of these superpowers and magical moments in therapy.

It is crucial to be proficient at calming during the EMDR processing phase. Identification of any calming thought can be amplified and intensified with a theme and party in my office. Kids love themes, as evidenced by the party industry. Any theme can be created with a puppet that amplifies your messages. When my daughter was 5 years old, she would often pretend to be a cat around the house, so we threw her a cat-themed birthday party. In my office, I adapted this theme by throwing a cat puppet party for a client, Sara, who loved cats. I put a loose collar on her neck and her cat puppet's neck with their names and little bells attached. Sara meowed across the floor with her cat puppet and then played cat games. The cat puppet threw tootsie rolls into a newly painted orange cardboard cat litter box that was layered with several inches of oatmeal. We ate candied fish tied to a fishing pole. A cat grooming station supplied hair bows for the cat's hair. A ball of yarn was unraveled with the joint effort of the child and cat puppet. A positive cognition, you deserve love, was printed inside the rolled ball of yarn. Sara relished in the calmness of being a cat, and through practice, was able to change her ego state from a disturbed state into a calming state.

Another time, flower puppets were the theme. Linda chose a pink rose puppet named Rose for the party. The flower puppets visited with Herman and discussed gardening tricks. Herman and Rose picked worms from the dirt together. Chocolate crumbs and gummy worms substituted for this activity. In another activity, Linda and Rose planted a real flower into a pot with Herman's help. Rose helped Linda blossom into a calm state and we all had fun at the same time.

The exercise "On the one hand... and then the other" (Mattise, as cited in Kaduson & Schaefer, 1997, p. 209) can be used as another puppet-based exercise to change ego states. This game inspired me to instruct children to alternate between two of their selected puppet characters. For example, a wise magician on one hand can talk to a lost baby bear on the other hand. The puppets on each hand talk to each other and create a self-dialogue. This interchange promotes an easy understanding of the changes of differing states. The magician represents the calm, collected, supportive ego state, and the lost baby bear plays the scared and sad ego state. Practicing alternative ego states with puppets prepares children to go from disturbed or scared to calm in their own lives.

Another technique used to help prepare children during phase two of EMDR is called "Parts Work." It allows the child to learn about the different "parts" of themselves to better understand themself. By learning and understanding the various parts of who we are, we develop more control over these parts. Examples of parts are:

- Emotional parts: sad, happy, guilty, scared, embarrassed.
- Characteristic parts: creative, procrastinator, funny, lazy, outgoing, listener.
- Role Parts: student, brother, cadet hamster mom, cub scout, daughter.
- Things children love to do parts: skier, artist, reader, hunter, dancer.
- Abilities: weight lifter, storyteller, mediator, protector, musician.
- Other descriptive parts that children identify with: Lego creator, friend, dreamer, loser, animal.

Fraser introduced this technique and named it the Dissociative Table. He explains that different "parts" are all sitting in a conference room at a meeting. Each part is introduced and understood. What is the part's role and what does it accomplish? The parts talk to each other and help each other in this exercise. "What does the angry part need, which part can help, and how?" Perhaps the mother part can approach the angry part and inquire about the anger and validate the angry part. Everyone has everything they need inside themselves to help themselves. Compassion is the key to helping each part and this becomes apparent during this exercise (McWilliams, 2011).

PAPT parts work is called, "Moo-Baa-Neigh". This technique takes place on a make believe farm. The child identifies with the parts and characteristics of the various animals he knows on the farm. Adaptions of this exercise can be a day at the zoo, a walk in the forest, or a swim in the ocean. Various types of puppets are required for the farm, zoo, forest, or ocean. With your imagination, any combination of puppets works well. Moo-Baa-Neigh Kits are available at www.ferniecouselling.ca.

The "Moo-Baa-Neigh" intervention is effective and three-dimensional. It accesses and taps into the child's unconscious mind, which provides the foundation for future understanding in problem solving. The use of puppets clearly demonstrates children's feelings about themselves, more so than words.

Barry, a 9-year-old boy, participated in Moo-Baa-Neigh in my play-room. We made a list of the various parts of himself that he identified with and chose animals from a farm to represent each part. The mouse represented his shy part, the chicken was the quiet caregiver part, a wise old owl for his student part, a duck for his swimming part, a horse for his work part, a baby goat was his playful part, and a bull for the angry part. We met all the parts (which are puppets) and learned what they did on the farm and how they helped at the farm. For example, the chicken was the mother hen part, she was caring and soft. She quietly sat on her eggs and patiently waited. The bull part was angry, charged the other animals, and spent most of his time alone in the field. We discussed the bull part and Barry identified that his bull part was charging. This created a problem on the farm as the other animals were afraid of him. Herman asked the bull puppet part why he charged, and he said he was protecting the farm. Then Herman asked who could help the bull part and Barry responded that the wise old owl part might help because he was wise and would know what to do to help with the anger. The wise old owl part suggested that the chicken part come over and explain to the bull part that she didn't need protection now that the chicken coop was safe. The baby goat part said he would help by coming over to the field and playing with the bull part. This play would help his loneliness and help him feel more included with the other farm animals. The bull part agreed that all the animals on the farm could help him with his charging problem if he opened up and made friends with the other animal parts. The parts represented by the different animal puppets exhibit compassion for the other animal parts.

To reiterate, this technique teaches children to accept and embrace all the parts of the self, including the parts that they view negatively. For instance, the role of the anxious part is to be fearful; being fearful helps us stay safe. The role of the sad part is to cry; crying relieves stress hormones that make us feel better. This powerful technique can be internalized to assist the child's compassion towards all parts of oneself.

The next step in the preparation phase is learning about and identifying the emotions, sensations, and cognitions that are stored in our memory systems when painful experiences occur. The emotions, sensations, and cognitions get stuck and are reset when the memories are processed. Children must be aware of and able to identify how their memories are stored in their thoughts, feelings, and body sensations (Shapiro, 2001).

The thoughts (cognitions) that have surfaced from the trauma are the first components to be addressed. This cognition identification and ownership can be effectively titrated using puppets. PAPT creates a distance between the child and memory. This makes the process easier for the child. A variety of puppets that the child chooses signify different messages and emotions.

PAPT is also a natural for learning the second component, where emotions are stored in our memory systems. Children must learn to identify each emotion and relate their feelings with the target memories requiring reset. Puppet play assists with emotional literacy. Feelings buttons in Herman the Turtle puppet's shell are useful. Teaching and identifying feelings by retrieving the buttons way down deep inside him without tickling him is challenging. The laughing from the tickles is contagious.

The third component deals with sensations. A child must be able to identify where they hold the feelings in their body and describe what it feels like. It is explained that when we have feelings, different things happen to our bodies. Puppets are great for helping children gain competency identifying body sensations and they can aid in recognizing and identifying experiential sensations from emotions.

My service dog, Betsy, helps me in my practice with children. I explain to children how dogs can be trained to sniff out health problems. I then introduce Rover, my sniffing dog puppet. In pretend play, he can sniff out the sensations with his powerful nose. When he sniffs out a body sensation or he is getting close to one, he barks. I then confer with the child and ask if that is where the sensation is occurring. The sky is the limit when a therapist uses their imagination to discover sensations. If therapists create their own puppets they can utilize noise boxes, sold by Build-A-Bear Workshop™, to insert into the puppets. Available inventory includes noise boxes that meow, bark, roar, and even allow for taping the therapist's own noises, voice, and messages.

The final components of a child's stuck memories are held in their thought patterns. These are referred to as negative cognitions. My Green Monster puppet is introduced to assist with identifying negative cognitions. I use the book *Don't Feed the Monster on Tuesdays!: The Children's Self-Esteem Book* by Adolph Moser (1991) to illustrate this concept. In this book there is a little green monster inside the child's head who "whispers awful things to us." When the monster begins his attacks, he is determined to make us feel bad about ourselves. He attacks using the negative cognitions. When my green monster puppet asks children if these cognitions are true, they can readily identify which cognitions fit for them.

Sometimes Peter the Pooper puppet revisits the session at this juncture and helps with his poopy cognitions. Many children say they feel weird when having these negative, confused thoughts. Peter can normalize them by validating their feelings and mentioning that many kids have the same feelings.

Buttons, similar to the feelings buttons, can be used for identifying the different sensations and cognitions learned. Buttons are easily made by hand or for sale at play therapy stores. Commercially sold buttons are called Kimochis Mixed Feeling Bags™ (www.kimochis.com/products/). This company sells several blank buttons to insert your own message. Cognition buttons, emotion buttons, and sensation buttons can all be used effectively. The child or the child's puppet can retrieve the buttons from the cotherapist puppet or other puppets in the playroom by a variety of means. The cotherapist puppet might be holding the emotion words, cognitions, and/or descriptions of the body sensations in a basket of cards, a hat with buttons, or written on pieces of felt and attached by Velcro to other props belonging to the puppet. For example, cognitions can be written on or attached to bananas that a monkey puppet retrieves.

Understanding and learning about negative beliefs that have developed from traumatic memory are necessary for change. These beliefs are what we tell ourselves when traumatic memory occurs. In order to help children replace negative cognitions (N/C) therapists counter them with positive cognitions (P/C). A list of negative cognitions is presented to identify their cognitive distortions.

Examples of negative cognitions include:

I'm worthless.
There is something wrong with me.

I am a bad person.
I'm dirty.
I am not loveable.

Shapiro, 2001, p. 60

The next skill is to teach and identify the positive cognitions that match the negative version of the thought. During the EMDR processing in phase two we turn the negative cognitions about ourselves into positive cognitions and reset the beliefs about ourselves from negative to positive. Examples of these positive cognitions are:

I did the best I could.
It's in the past.
I learned from it.
I'm in control.
I'm lovable.
I'm a good person.
I now have choices.

Shapiro, 2001, p. 60

Following the learning of cognitions, the identification of target memories is required for processing the trauma experiences. PAPT suggests identifying targets by utilizing the help of a cotherapist puppet. This provides an additional layer of distance. The cotherapist puppet can question other puppets. This may reveal other repressed targets necessary for processing.

Examples of questions to ask a child (or a child's puppet if they are holding one) in order to uncover additional targets are:

- "Why does this ostrich have his head in the sand?"
- "What made the skunk ready to spray?"
- "Why is the dragon ready to breathe fire?"
- "Why is the deer frozen in the road?"
- "Why does the bully lion attack?"
- "Who is the porcupine afraid of? Is that why his quills are out?"

Different puppets can elicit a plethora of emotions and cognitions.

To take this exercise one step further, the therapist repeats the practice of identifying thoughts, feelings, and body sensations. This repetition helps solidify the process of identification which is a paramount aspect of the processing phase.

Herman asks the child's puppets: "Do you ever feel like that?" Then continue with, "What is he feeling?" (recognizing emotion) or, "What does he think?" (negative cognitions) or, "How would these animals prefer to feel?" (positive cognitions). Children should be competent with the identification of emotions, sensations and cognitions prior to moving on to the next phase.

Phase three of EMDR is described by Shapiro (2001) as "Identifying the components of each target and establishing a baseline response before processing begins" (p. 132). The target is the memory chosen for processing. "The various components of the target memory are the individualized experience, sight, image, or picture the child has of the target, the feelings that transpired during the target, the body sensations that occurred when the target memory was experienced, and the corresponding negative cognitions. EMDR refers to this list as TICES (Target, Image, Cognitions, Emotions, Sensations)" (Shapiro, 2001). This assessment phase can be performed utilizing all the PAPT techniques mentioned earlier in the learning and preparation phases in order to assess each target.

The goal is to identify the emotions that occur with the target, identify the sensations that are held in the child's body regarding the target, identify the negative cognitions that are the result of the target, and then formulate a positive cognition to replace the negative cognition.

In the assessment phase, after the child is asked to recall the memory, the therapist asks them to assess or rate the disturbance level of that target using the SUD Scale (Subjective Unit of Distress Scale). Zero represents neutral intensity and ten equals the highest possible anxiety.

Once again, puppets aid in this stage of EMDR. The Subjective Unit of Distress can be measured by the child using their puppet. A puppet can go to a large scale placed on the floor, and "step" [with the child] on the corresponding number between 0 and 10 of their distress levels. I made a scale from a white vinyl tablecloth using happy, sad, and neutral faces. White vinyl can easily be purchased at any fabric store.

The child is then asked to identify a negative thought or belief that pertains to the chosen target selected. Following the identification of the negative cognition, the child is asked to verbalize a positive thought or belief (a positive cognition) they would like to have about themselves to replace the negative cognition. The positive cognition is the direct opposite of the negative cognition. A phrase such as "I am worthless" is converted to, "I am worthwhile". The flip side of "I am out of control" is "I am in control". "I did something wrong" is converted to "I did the best I could".

Next, the child is asked to rate how true they feel this positive belief is by means of the VOC Scale (Validity of Cognition). Number

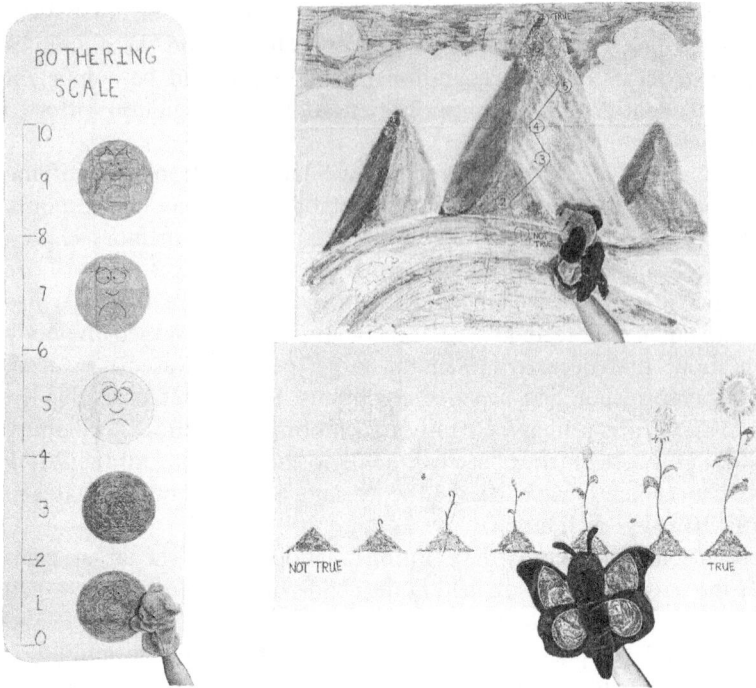

Figure 14.2 VOC and SUD scales

1 represents completely false and number 7 is completely true. If the child says "I am worthless" when he identifies the N/C from the target memory, the therapist asks the child to rate the P/C that was created to counter the N/C. If the P/C was, "I am worthwhile", then the therapist asks, "How true is it that you are worthwhile?" The validity of cognition can be demonstrated by moving the child's puppet to the appropriate number between 1 and 7 on the scale.

Throughout the processing phase the child is asked to reevaluate the SUD (Subjective Unit of Distress) of the target memory being processed. This gives the child an opportunity to break from processing and get up and move around with their puppet so they can regain focus. It also allows the child time to experience the memory as its disturbance level decreases.

I have several scales in my playroom to measure SUD and VOC. These scales include Climb the Mountain, The Flower Blossom, and Hot! Hot! Hot!, which either hang on the wall or lie on the floor. When using the flower blossom scale, the goal is to reach to the beautiful blossoming flower.

When hung on the wall they are played like pin the tail on the donkey. The children's puppets play this game by indicating the intensity of their experience(s) by pointing to the corresponding number on the scale. When the scale is on the floor, the puppet sits on the number correlating to the intensity of the memory. Scale pictures can be modified to address the child's interests. Weather/temperature scales illustrate pictures beginning with gray clouds to bright sun, puppies to grown dogs, and more.

As mentioned before, phases four through eight of EMDR must be practiced by a mental health professional with expertise and training in this modality. To ensure safety and ethics, only brief information on the value of puppets in these phases will be discussed in the following paragraphs.

In EMDR phase four, eye-movement desensitization and reprocessing is implemented. PAPT is helpful in explaining EMDR to children. When children preview an EMDR puppet session their anxiety levels are diminished. This concept was presented as *Medical Puppet Play* (Landreth, 2002), earlier in the book.

PAPT offers many effective strategies for desensitization and reprocessing as well. This is accomplished by bilateral stimulation (BLS) and can be easily performed by the cotherapist puppet. "Bilateral stimulation that provides alternative dual attention stimuli can be implemented with several methods. Eye movements, taps, tones, and even drumming produce this effect. These alternative stimuli may contribute to EMDR's therapeutic effect by maintaining the client's simultaneous external awareness during a period of internal stress or by activating brain functions inherent in the movements or the attention paid to two simultaneously present stimuli" (Shapiro, 2001).

Herman the Turtle puppet uses a blinking sword to perform this bilateral stimulation. He waves his sword back and forth in front of the child's eyes, tracking their eyes quickly to produce rapid eye movements. Hand puppets or finger puppets can be used alone for tracking. These eye movements resemble the same movements in REM sleep that aid in processing or digesting information and memories. A magician puppet can use a magic wand, a conductor can use his baton, a drummer can use a drumstick, a dog can use a bone, a rabbit a carrot, a witch a broom, and a baseball player a bat, etc.

Installation, phase five, concentrates on the full integration of a positive self-assessment with the targeted information (Shapiro, 2001, p. 160). This is accomplished by slow, short bilateral stimulation paired with the positive cognition. A puppet show can reinforce this new positive way of thinking and being.

Effective installation tools, similar to the puppets used for processing, can be found in a therapist's menagerie of puppets. For example, one puppet in my playroom used for installation is a leaf. One intervention found in Liana Lowenstien's (2002) book *More Creative Interventions for Troubled Children and Youth* is called "Turn over a New Leaf" (p. 102). This game inspired the creation of a leaf puppet. The leaf puppet is used to install the positive cognitions. One side of the leaf has a negative cognition and the other side a positive cognition. Once the child has turned over his cognition, he can turn over a new leaf. Velcro is used to attach the cognition to felt on each side of the leaf. Once identified, the child can hold up the old cognition and validate his new cognition. A felt heart can be attached with Velcro on the positive cognition side of the leaf. Then bilteral stimulation, slow, short sets, will assist with installation of this new positive cognition.

The body scan is the sixth phase of EMDR. This phase reexamines whether body sensations continue to exist after the desensitization occurs. My dog puppet, Rover, returns to the playroom and continues his duties of sniffing out the sensations.

Phase seven, closure, is a step that allows time to close the session with explanations and to answer the child's questions so the child can leave the playroom in a positive frame of mind. To facilitate this phase, Herman the Turtle will ask the child to go on his adventure trip to the sea again and swim with his turtle friends in order to produce a calm ego state to end the session.

During the closing phase of EMDR it is often suggested a child create a container in which to deposit his traumatic memories. Puppets can serve the same purpose by taking and holding these memories. A racoon puppet has a trashcan that he uses to keep the yucky memories in the trash until next session. Many other puppets can also be used to create containment. My rabbit puppet has a magic hat that can store memories, my postman puppet has a mailbox, the genie puppet has a lamp, the enchanted tree has a hole in it, and my bear puppet's vest has a pocket. Puppets that have zippers are effective. Closing the puppet stage curtain also helps with closure. These are just a few ideas to help children pretend to put away the memories into the container and leave them behind.

Re-evaluation, phase eight, usually occurs at the following session. If the process is complete, the child's disturbance will no longer be present. If the disturbance is still present, phases four through seven are repeated.

PAPT is an effective tool to enhance EMDR with children. The combination of PAPT and EMDR can be turned into a fun, safe, and enchanted therapy treatment that converts a child's frightening, painful, and difficult processes into a healing and transformative experience. PAPT, combined with EMDR, is a sublime fit for children.

Conclusion

PAPT began with Herman; the turtle, my cotherapist puppet. He created a magic place for healing that children refer to as "Herman's House". When children and families meet Herman, their eyes light up and their hearts melt. Using puppets produces a powerful connection and trust needed for the therapeutic process. This book shared how through puppets, effective interventions address any theoretical platform you choose to work from. It includes history, research interventions, case studies, the art of puppetry, and the worldwide benefits of puppet-assisted play therapy. The unique ideas presented will enhance your knowledge and creativity which will make your therapy thrive and ultimately be more rewarding.

I hope you not only enjoyed this book, but gained an abundance of new ideas, skills, and strategies to help with children's healing in your playroom. PAPT is an ever-growing avenue to reach out to children in therapy. Kids love it and with your expanded imagination and creativity, you too will be encouraged to further embrace the art of puppetry. PAPT is an amazing, gratifying, and entertaining modality that incorporates the magic of healing with the power of puppets.

Your new cotherapist puppet will be an asset to your work, family, and friends. They are easy to train and fun to have in your office. Working together, your cotherapist puppet will most likely teach you a great deal and spark your talents in ways you never dreamed. Hats off to you and your cotherapist for working with children who need and benefit from your help!

Figure C.1 The end

Appendix A: Original Research

Can puppetry enhance creativity and why is that important in mental health?

Abstract

Creativity, play, and puppetry are crucial for children's healthy development. Puppetry is an excellent avenue to provide this experience. Benefits gleaned from creativity are; positive personal perceptions, problem-solving skills, conflict resolution skills, academic ability, coping skills, critical thinking skills, and social affective domains.

This research project examined creativity enhancement in the classroom through a standardized test called the Torrance Test for Creative Thinking (Torrance, 1990). Creativity or divergent thinking, namely verbal fluency, flexibility, and originality, was measured among third and fourth grade students. A creative puppetry curriculum of eight sessions was implemented and a posttest was then administered. Results were derived from the difference between pre and posttests. Definitions of creativity and research on various areas of creativity, including benefits, measurements, attitudes, play, and puppetry, are discussed. Findings reveal positive outcomes with promising results of creativity enhancement. Differences between the sexes were also observed as well as the differing class grades. Evidence indicates that creativity may be enhanced through puppetry. Future studies of creativity enhancement programs may prove to be a critical component for optimal mental health in the classroom.

Creativity Puppet Curriculum

This curriculum was implemented with my ventriloquist puppet, Bear-niece.

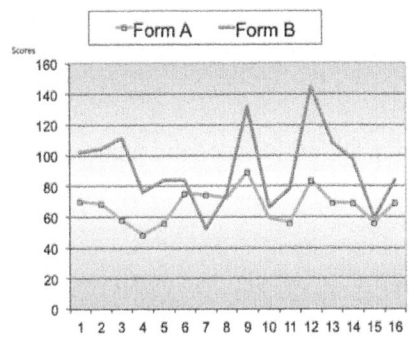

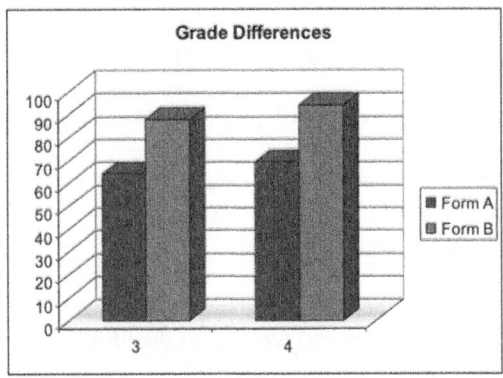

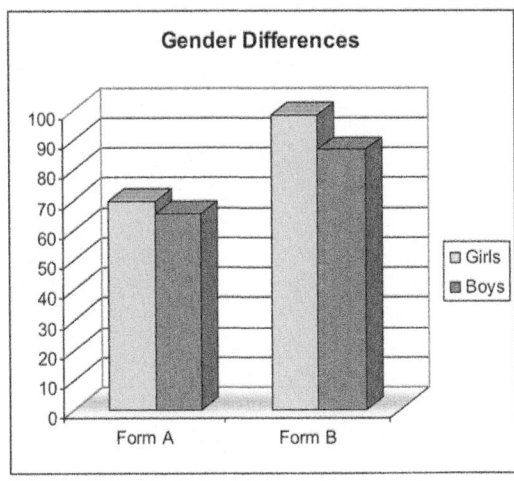

PRE-TEST   POST TEST

Figure A.1 Torrance Tests research results

Components of this curriculum were presented to the students to learn and have fun with puppets. Constructing puppets, exercises, games, stories, and puppet shows were incorporated in this study. The topics covered included:

- Brainstorming: learning about the rules and methods
- Convergent thinking: learning about and discussing the fallacy of having one right answer
- Divergent thinking: eliciting many different answers
- I am special: honor each individual's own creativity
- I am creative: teaching about the self-fulfilling prophecy, believing in oneself, describing how everyone has different talents and is creative in different ways
- Conformity and challenging the rules – being silly: thinking differently
- Getting support: fear blocks creativity, elicit others' encouragement and ideas
- Combining two ideas to make a third
- How to use a random word to solve a problem.
- Look from a different perspective or view.

Ask the 5 W questions: what, when, where, why, and how to expand on an idea while adding the five senses and feelings to the idea.

Appendix B: JOANN's Puppet Pattern

Other puppets

Bryan the Brain, Peter the Pooper, and the Green Monster puppets are created and designed by Cheryl Hulburd and are available for purchase at www.ferniecounselling.ca.

All Folkmanis Puppets are available as well. They can be purchased at www.ferniecounselling.ca.

Figure A.2 JOANN's puppet pattern – puppets made by C. Hulburd

SUPPLIES & TOOLS:

- 12"x20" fleece for each puppet body
- Fleece for eyes, noses, whiskers, paws
- Sewing machine
- Basics sewing supplies
- Small black buttons
- Tacky glue or low-temp hot glue gun & glue sticks
- Pinking shears

DIRECTIONS:

FOR ALL PUPPETS:

1. Enlarge patterns to measurements noted. Cut two layers of fleece from main puppet shape for each character.
2. Cut corresponding details for each puppet.

CAT & BUNNY:

1. Double layer the ears for stability. Sew ears together. Tack the inside of the ear to outer ear with glue.
2. Pin ears onto the main puppet body.
3. Sandwich the ears with the other layer of the body. Sew along the edge of puppet, leaving the bottom open.
4. Glue on whiskers, nose, paws and eyes.

ONE-EYED MONSTER:

1. Cut one layer of the fur with pinking shears.
2. Cut contrasting color of main puppet body with pinking shears.
3. Sew along the edge of puppet, leaving the bottom open.
4. Glue on eye.

LION:

1. Cut one 10"x4" piece of fleece for the mane. Fold mane in half lengthwise and baste the open long side. Cut fringe along folded edge of fleece, stopping at the basting stitches.
2. Pin mane to the inside of the puppet along the edge of the face. Sandwich the mane with the other layer of the body. Sew along the edge of puppet, leaving the bottom open.
3. Glue on eyes, nose, mouth and paws.

TURTLE:

1. Cut two layers of the shell. With contrasting thread, add details to the shell.
2. Sew main puppet body together.
3. Glue on shell and eyes.

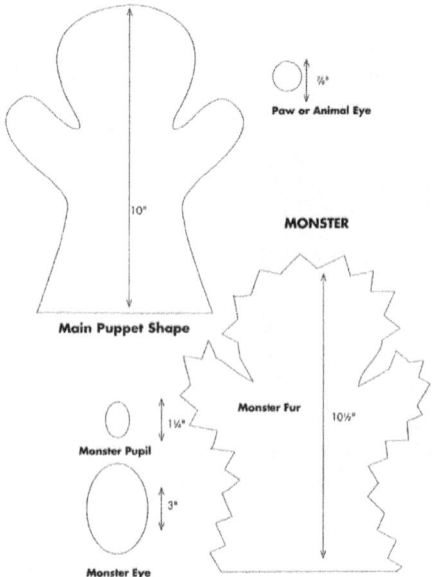

Figure A.2 (continued)

Bibliography

AddictionInfo. (n.d.). *Stages of change model.* Retrieved from www. addictioninfo.org/articles/11/1/Stages-of-Change-Model/Page1.html

Axline, M. V. (1947). *Play therapy.* New York, NY: Ballantine Books.

Badenoch, B. (2008). *Being a brain-wise therapist.* New York, NY: W.W. Norton & Co.

Bandura, A. (1975). The ethics and social purposes of behavior modification. In C. M. Franks & G. T. Wilson (Eds.), *Annual review of behavior therapy theory and practice* (Vol. 3). New York, NY: Brunner/Mazel.

Barnard, K. E., & Brazelton, T. B. (Eds.). (1990). *Clinical infant reports. Touch: The foundation of experience: Full revised and expanded proceedings of Johnson & Johnson Pediatric Round Table X.* Madison, CT: International Universities Press.

Berkowitz, L. (1993). *Aggression: Its causes, consequences, and control.* New York, NY: McGraw-Hill.

Bernard, J. M., & Goodyear, R. K. (2009). *Fundamentals of clinical supervision* (4th ed.). Upper Saddle River, NJ: Pearson.

Blumenthal, E. (2005). *Puppetry: A world history.* New York, NY: Harry N. Abrams.

Booth, P. B., & Jernberg, A. M. (2010). *Theraplay: Helping parents and children build better relationships through attachment-based play* (3rd ed.). San Francisco, CA: Jossey-Bass.

Bow, J. N. (1993). Overcoming resistance. In C. E. Schaefer (Ed.), *The therapeutic powers of play* (pp. 17–40). Northvale, NJ: Jason Aronson.

Bowlby, J. (1988). *A secure attachment.* New York, NY: Routledge.

Bratton, S., Landreth, G., Kellam, T., & Blackard, S.R. (2006). *Child–parent relationship therapy (CPRT) treatment manual.* New York, NY: Routledge.

Brody, V. A. (1997). *Dialogue of touch: Developmental play therapy.* London: Rowman and Littlefield.

Bushman, B. J. (2002). Does venting anger feed or extinguish the flame? Catharsis, rumination, distraction, anger and aggressive responding. *Personality and Social Psychology Bulletin, 28*(6), 724–731. doi:10.1177/0146167202289002

Cangelosi, D. (2012). To direct or not to direct: That is the question. *Play Therapy, 7*(2), 20–22.

Child Protection Resource. (n.d.). *What is attachment theory? Why is it important?* https://childprotectionresource.online/what-is-attachment-theory-why-is-it-important/

Cognitive behavioral therapy. (2019). In *Wikipedia.* en.wikipedia.org/wiki/Cognitive_behavioral_therapy

Compton, B. R., & Galaway, B. (1999). *Social work processes* (6th ed.). Belmont, CA: Brooks/Cole.

Courtney, J. A., & Siu, A. F. Y. (2018). Practitioner experiences of touch in working with children in play therapy. *International Journal of Play Therapy, 27*(2), 92–102.

Davidson, R. J., Kabat-Zinn, J., Schumacher, J., Rosenkranz, M., Muller, D., Santorelli, S. F., ... Sheridan, J. F. (2003). Alterations in brain and immune function produced by mindfulness meditation. *Psychosomatic Medicine, 65*(4), 564–570.

Davis, N. (1996). *Once upon a time: Therapeutic stories that teach and heal.* Self-published.

Dinkmeyer, D. C., Dinkmeyer, D. C., Jr., & Sperry, L. (1987). *Adlerian counseling and psychotherapy* (2nd ed.). Columbus, OH: Merrill Publishing.

Drewes, A. A. (2008). Bobo revisited: What the research says. *International Journal of Play Therapy, 17*(1), 52–65.

Drews, A. A., & Schafer, C. E. (2018). *Puppet play therapy.* New York, NY: Routledge.

Dunham, J. (n.d.). Meet Achmed the Dead Terrorist. Spark of Insanity. https://youtu.be/GBvfiCdk-jc

Ego State Therapy International. (n.d.). www.egostateinternational.com/

Findling, J. H., Bratton, S. C., & Henson, R. K. (2006). Development of the trauma play scale: An observation-based assessment of the impact of trauma on play therapy behaviors of young children. *International Journal of Play Therapy, 15*(1), 7–36. doi:10.1037/h0088906

Fisher, R. (2006). Still thinking: The case for meditation with children. *Thinking Skills and Creativity, 1*(2), 146–151. doi:10.1016/j.tsc.2006.06.004

Fraser, G. (2003). Fraser's dissociative table technique. *Journal of Trauma and Dissociation, 4*, 5–8. doi:10.1300/J229v04n04_02

Geen, R. G., & Quanty, M. B. (1977). The catharsis of aggression: An evaluation of a hypothesis. In L. Berkowitz (Ed.), *Advances in experimental social psychology* (Vol. 10, pp. 1–37). New York, NY: Academic Press.

Gendler, M. (1986). Group puppetry with school-age children: Rationale, procedure and therapeutic implications. *The Arts in Psychotherapy, 13*(1), 45–52. doi:10.1016/0197-4556(86)90007-9

Gomez, A. (2009). *Thought kits for kids.* www.anagomez.org/node/156

Gomez, A. (2013). *EMDR therapy and adjunct approaches with children: Complex trauma attachment and dissociation.* New York, NY: Springer.

Gomez, A. (2018). *Stories and storytellers: The thinking mind, the heart, and the body.* Evanston, IL: Agate.

GoodTherapy. (n.d.a). *Object relations.* www.goodtherapy.org/learn-about-therapy/types/object-relations

GoodTherapy. (n.d.b). *Window of tolerance.* www.goodtherapy.org/blog/psychpedia/window-of-tolerance

Gowan, J. C., Demos, G. D., & Torrance, E. P. (1967). *Creativity: Its educational implications.* Hoboken, NJ: John Wiley & Sons.

Harris, R. (n.d.). Mindfulness skills (Volume 1). *Act Mindfully.* Retrieved from www.actmindfully.com.au/product/mindfulness-skills-volume-1-mp3-instant-download/

Harrison, J. (1994). *Dear Bear.* New York, NY: HarperCollins.

Haworth, M. R. (1968). Doll play and puppetry. In A. I. Rabin (Ed.), *Projective techniques in personality assessment* (pp. 327–365). New York, NY: Springer.

Healing Couples Retreats. (n.d.). *Full spectrum.* Retrieved from https://healingcouplesretreats.com/card/full-spectrum/

Hynes, A. M., & Hynes-Berry, M. (1994). *Biblio/poetry therapy, the interactive process. A handbook.* St. Cloud, MN: North Star Press.

Irwin, E. C. (1985). Puppets in Therapy: an assessment procedure. *American Journal of Psychotherapy, 39*(3).

Irwin, E. C., & Shapiro, M. I. (1975). Puppetry as a diagnostic and therapeutic technique. *Psychiatry and Art, 4*(1), 86–94.

Kaduson, H., & Schaefer, C. (1997). *101 favorite play therapy techniques.* London: Rowman and Littlefield.

Kaduson, H., & Schaefer, C. (2004). *101 favorite play therapy techniques.* London: Rowman and Littlefield.

Karst, P. (2000). *The invisible string.* Camarillo, CA: DeVorss & Co.

Kasza, K. (1992). *A mother for Choco.* New York, NY: Putnam and Sons.

Kermit the Frog. (2019, December 17). In *Wikipedia.* en.wikipedia.org/w/index.php?title=Kermit_the_Frog&oldid=931246667

Knipe, J. (2010). Back of the head scale. In M. Luber (Ed.), *EMDR scripted protocols.* (pp. 233–234). New York, NY: Springer.

Kottman, T., & Meany-Walen, K. (2016). *Partners in play: An Adlerian approach to play therapy* (3rd ed.). Washington, DC: American Counseling Association.

Landreth, G. (2001). *Innovations in play therapy.* New York, NY: Brunner/Routledge.

Landreth, G. (2002). *The art of play therapy.* New York, NY: Brunner/Routledge.

Loftin, S. (2018). Bring play to the patient: Bedside sessions in a hospital setting. *Play Therapy, 13*(4).

Lowenstein, L. (2002). *More creative interventions for troubled children and youth.* Toronto, CA: Champion Press.

Lowenstein, L. (2008). *Assessment and treatment activities for children, adolescents, and families: Practitioners share their most effective techniques.* Toronto, CA: Champion Press.

Luber, M. (2010). *EMDR scripted protocols.* New York, NY: Springer.

MacLean, K. L. (2004). *Peaceful piggy meditation.* Park Ridge, IL: Albert Whitman & Co.

MacLean, K. L. (2009). *Moody cow meditates.* Somerville, MA: Wisdom Publications.

McWilliams, N. (2011). *Psychoanalytic diagnosis: Understanding personality structure in the clinical process.* New York, NY: Guilford Press.

Malkin, M. (1977). *Traditional and folk puppets of the world.* South Brunswick, NJ: A.S. Barnes.

McGlone, F., Wessberg, J., & Olausson, H. (2014). Discriminative and affective touch: Sensing and feeling. *Neuron, 82*(4), 737–755. doi:10.1016/j.neuron.2014.05.001

Mills, J. C., & Crowley, R. J. (1986). *Therapeutic metaphors for children and the child within.* London: Routledge.

Moser, A. (1991). *Don't feed the monster on Tuesdays!: The children's self-esteem book.* Kansas City, MO: Landmark Editions.

Norton, C., & Norton, B. (1997). *Reaching children through play therapy: An experiential approach.* Denver, CO: White Apple.

Oaklander, V. (1978). *Windows to our children.* Boulder, CO: Real People Press.

Oberoi, A. (2014). The science of storytelling & memory and their impact on CRO. *CXL Institute.* https://cxl.com/blog/the-science-of-storytelling-memory-motivation-and-its-impact-on-cro/

O'Conner, K. J. (2000). *Play therapy primer: Theories and techniques.* Hoboken, NJ: John Wiley & Sons.

Paul, G. L. (1967). Strategy of outcome research in psychotherapy. *Journal of Consulting Psychology, 31*(2), 109–118.

Pehrsson, E. (2006). Benefits of utilizing bibliotherapy within play therapy. *Play Therapy, 1*(2), 10–14.

Philpott, A. R. (1977). *Puppets and therapy.* Boston: Plays, Inc.

Piaget, J. (1952). *The origins of intelligence in children.* New York, NY: International University Press.

Piper, W. (1930). *The little engine that could.* New York, NY: Platt & Monk Publishers.

Play therapy. (2019). In *Wikipedia.* en.wikipedia.org/wiki/Play_therapy

Psychodynamic psychotherapy. (2019). In *Wikipedia.* en.wikipedia.org/wiki/Psychodynamic_psychotherapy

Rasmussen, G., & Rasmussen, T. (1997). *Loosen up: Quick activities to build confidence and creativity.* Eugene, OR: Tin Man Press.

Ross, T. (2002). *Eggbert, the slightly cracked egg.* London: Penguin.

Runco, M. A. (2004). Creativity. *Annual Review of Psychology, 55,* 657.

Saenz, M. (2002). *Powerful puppetry.* New Bern, NC: Marco Products.

SARK. (2004). *Make your creative dreams real.* New York, NY: Fireside.

Schaefer, C. E. (2018). The 10 basic principles of prescriptive play therapy. *Play Therapy, 13*(4), 24–27.

Shapiro, F. (2001). *Eye movement desensitization and reprocessing: Basic principles, protocols and procedures (EMDR).* New York, NY: Guilford Press.

Shazer, S. (1988). www.brief-stategic-family-therapy.com

Sheppard, C. H. (1998). *Brave Bart: A story for traumatized and grieving children.* Albion, MI: National Institute for Trauma and Loss in Children.

Siegel, D. (1999). *The developing mind: How relationships and the brain interact to shape who we are.* New York, NY: Guilford Press.

Siegel, D., & Bryson, T. (2011). *The whole brain child: 12 revolutionary strategies to nurture your child's developing mind.* New York, NY: Random House.

Siegel, D., & Hartzell, M. (2003). *Parenting from the inside out: How a deeper self-understanding can help you raise children who thrive.* New York, NY: J.P. Tarcher/Putnam.

Smith, P. K., Smees, R., & Pellegrini, A. D. (2004). Play fighting and real fighting: Using video playback methodology with young children. *Aggressive Behavior, 30*(2), 164–173.

Sparks, R. (1993). *The heart of self-esteem.* Vancouver, BC: Roger Sparks & Associates.

Spitz, R. A., & Wolf, K. M. (1946). Anaclitic depression: An inquiry into the genesis of psychiatric conditions in early childhood, II. *The Psychoanalytic Study of the Child, 2*, 313–342.

Sprunk, T. P., Mitchell, J. A., Myrow, D., & O'Connor, K. (2001). Paper on touch: Clinical, professional, and ethical issues. *Association for Play Therapy.* https://cdn.ymaws.com/www.a4pt.org/resource/resmgr/Publications/ Paper_ On_Touch.pdf

Steffy, L. (2010). *Shelly's shell.* Renfrew, Ontario: General Store Publishing House.

Stern, C. (1999). Gates of repentance. *The New Union Prayerbook for the Days of Awe.* New York, NY: Central Conference of America.

Stutey, D. M., Dunn, M., Shelnut, J., & Ryan, J. B. (2017). Impact of Adlerian play therapy on externalizing behaviors of at-risk preschoolers. *International Journal of Play Therapy, 26*(4), 196–206.

Sweeney, T. J. (2009). *Adlerian counseling and psychotherapy: A practitioner's approach.* New York, NY: Taylor & Francis.

Sweeney, D. S., & Homeyer, L. (1999). *Group puppetry: The handbook of group play therapy. How to do it, how it works, whom its best for.* San Francisco, CA: Jossey-Bass.

Terr, L. (2008). *Magical moments of change: How psychotherapy turns kids around.* New York, NY: W.W. Norton & Co.

Torrance, E. P. (1990). *Torrance tests of creative thinking.* Bensenville, IL: Scholastic Testing Service.

Turner, F. (1996). *Social work treatment: Interlocking theoretical approaches* (4th ed.). New York, NY: The Free Press.

VW Corporation. Fun theory study: www.youtube.com/results?search_ query=vw+fun+theory

Warren, R., & Kurlychek, R. T. (1981). Treatment of maladaptive anger and aggression: Catharsis vs behavior therapy. *Corrective & Social Psychiatry & Journal of Behavior Technology, Methods & Therapy, 27*(3), 135–139.

Weedn, F., & Weedn, L. (1995). *The enchanted tree: An original American tale.* San Rafael, CA: Cedco Publishing.

Widrich, L. (2012, December 5). The science of storytelling: Why telling a story is the most powerful way to activate our brains. *Lifehacker.* https://lifehacker. com/the-science-of-storytelling-why-telling-a-story-is-the-5965703

Williams, M. L., & O'Quinn Burke, D. (2007). *Cool cats, calm kids: Relaxation and stress management for young people.* Atascadero, CA: Impact Publishers.

Woltmann, A. G. (1940). The use of puppets in understanding children. *Mental Hygiene, 24*, 445–458.

Woltmann, A. G. (1951). The use of puppetry as a projective method in therapy. In G. L. Anderson (Ed.), *An introduction to projective techniques.* New York, NY: Prentice Hall.

Index